Biblical Parenting

Millennial Mind Publishing
2389 South, 300 East, Salt Lake City, Utah 84115
www.american-book.com

Printed in the United States of America on acid-free paper.

Biblical Parenting

Designed by Stacy Swartz, suswartz@thiel.edu

Publisher's Note: *This publication is designed to provide accurate and authoritative information in regard to the subject matter covered. It is sold or distributed with the understanding that the publisher and author is not engaged in rendering legal, accounting, or other professional service. If legal advice or other expert assistance is required, the services of a competent professional person in a consultation capacity should be sought.*

Library of Congress Cataloging-in-Publication Data is available upon request.

ISBN 1-930586-68-X

Lutton, Crystal, Biblical Parenting

Special Sales

These books are available at special discounts for bulk purchases. Special editions, including personalized covers, excerpts of existing books, and corporate imprints, can be created in large quantities for special needs. For more information e-mail cln@american-book.com or call 1-800-296-1248.

Biblical Parenting

Crystal Lutton

Dedication

I wish to dedicate this book to my husband William and our two children Liam and Fiona, the three people who have made me a mother and helped me become the mother that I am.

Foreword

Christian parents have been accustomed to thinking about discipline as punishment – something you do *to* a child rather than something you do *with* a child. However, discipline is more about developing the right relationship with your child rather than the right techniques. Throughout this book you will learn how the "rod verses" are grossly misinterpreted, and that you don't have to spank your child to be a godly parent. Besides there being no biblical basis for spanking, in my thirty years in pediatric practice I have rarely seen spanking work. Instead, it creates a distance between parent and child, plants a seed of anger (and sometimes violence) in the child, and often tends to worsen a child's behavior. It is also interesting that the "rod verses" are only mentioned in the Old Testament. In the New Testament, Christ taught a gentler approach, as stated by Paul in 1 Corinthians 4:21: "Shall I come to you with the rod, or in love and with a gentle spirit?"

Throughout this book you will learn that discipline is creating an attitude within the child and an atmosphere in the home that makes spanking unnecessary. Scripture is clear that parents are to be authority figures for their children. Yet, authority begins with developing a mutual trust between parent and child: "Train up a child in the way he should go, and when he is old he will not depart." (Proverbs 22:6) This implies that parents know the individual bent of their child. To teach your child to trust you, and to become an expert in your child, begins with practicing a style of parenting we call *attachment parenting*. Throughout this book you will learn how this style of parenting helps you get behind the eyes of your child and direct behavior from within rather than applying force on the outside. Attachment parenting will help you teach your child how to develop inner controls. You will also learn that attachment parenting does not mean permissive parenting. On the contrary, one of the "B's" (in addition to the other B's of birth bonding, breastfeeding, babywearing, belief in baby's cries, and bedding close to baby) is balance – knowing when to say "yes" and when to say "no." Attachment parenting implies a balance between meeting the child's needs and also saving enough energy to meet the needs of your marriage. Finally, it is my hope that in reading this book parents will discover the true joy of living with a well-disciplined child.

-- Dr. William Sears, author of *The Complete Book of Christian Parenting and Childcare*

Preface

Crystal Lutton's small book is big in insights and practical suggestions. Thanks to the training and example of her own godly mother, Crystal has devoted much thought and prayer to parenting principles that are biblical, practical, and also kind. In the words of Hebrews 10:24, this book will spur Christian parents "on toward love and good deeds" toward their own children, so that those children will, in turn, love and serve both God and others. Crystal offers a much-needed voice to an important contemporary discussion.

Chapter One
An Introduction

Let me say up front that my heart is for children and young families. I grew up in a home with a mother and father who had not been taught good parenting. Unfortunately, the only skills we have for parenting come from the way we were parented, unless we get them from somewhere else, so I'm sure that their parents were not taught good skills either. But my parents loved the Lord and were committed to raising me in the knowledge of who He is and what that means to our lives.

It was very important to my parents that my mother be a stay-at-home mom, which was not popular in the 1970's. So I had a mother at home and no designer clothes when most of my friends had the opposite. There were three of us children, my two younger brothers and I, and my mother struggled in her parenting of us. By the time my youngest brother came along, my mother had learned about La Leche League. La Leche League is an international organization that is devoted to supporting the mother and baby in a breastfeeding relationship. They provide breastfeeding support in the form of monthly meetings, educational seminars, community classes, and through providing sales of Over the Shoulder Baby Holder slings for baby wearing (a basic element of attachment parenting) and breast pumps. They love women and babies and are deeply committed to spreading the truth that breastfeeding is best for babies (even the formula companies have to admit that) and that nearly every woman can breastfeed with the right education and support. My mother joined LLL and became a leader after having my youngest brother. But even with support in these areas of parenting she still struggled with other skills.

My mother couldn't believe that what she had been taught and what was still being taught in her Christian circles could possibly be the way God intended us to parent. So she cried out to God for two years, begging Him to show her what she was doing wrong, asking His guidance. He woke her in the middle of the night and revealed to her what she'd been longing to learn. She treasured these teachings in her heart, implemented them with her children, and hoped to someday write a book to share His message with others. God warned her that the Christian community was not ready to receive the message yet and when she shared with someone without the Lord's leading they were not interested. She learned quickly and over the last twenty years she has shared only with those whom God has told her to share. They have been blessed and it has changed their entire attitude about parenting. I learned what God showed my mother through being her child and through hearing her share it with others.

While my mother still lacked skills for much of what God had shown her, God has taken me on a path where I have learned many of the skills for implementing the paradigm shift He showed her that night. I worked with children in many settings and finally was given the opportunity to mentor under Lisa Kuzara Seibold, Minister of Early Childhood Education at Word of Grace church in Mesa, Arizona. She is a true woman of God who is connected with God's heart for children. Under her tutelage I learned many of the skills that I will share with you. It is from her that I was introduced to the ideas of reflecting and validating feelings and the 5 Steps, which she developed. It was wonderful to be immersed in such a beautiful, Godly, Grace-Based Discipline environment and to not only learn these skills but to see them work with each and every child. I am especially grateful to Lisa for embracing me in the spirit of Grace-Based Discipline and providing me an environment to learn more about myself and my calling. I am a first-hand testament to the fact that relationships of Grace-Based Discipline provide a safe place for an individual to grow in their understanding of and relationship to the Lord— regardless of their age.

I have also developed many practical skills with the members of an online Christian Attachment Parenting List emphasizing non-punitive discipline. This group was started by my dear friend Joanne Davidson and came about at a time when I really had to work out the specifics of Grace-Based Discipline in my own home. Joanne is a beautiful woman whose path to Grace-Based Discipline has paralleled mine. We have been able to provide each other with support and ideas as we've grown in our understanding of the gifts God has given us. The online list she started came out of our search for other like-minded parents and is the first of its kind to provide support for Christians who practice attachment parenting and desire that attached beginning to flow into a relationship of Grace-Based Discipline. While the foundation of attachment parenting is wonderful for developing relationship between parent and child, around the age of 18 months a child requires more active discipline. It is at this age that many who practice AP with their infants feel helpless to parent and turn to more punitive styles for help, or do nothing and slip into a permissive mindset. Not only have the women and men I've come to know in this community provided me with support and encouragement, but they have given me the opportunity to hone the skills I will be sharing here and to create new ones to situations I hadn't yet encountered. Joanne, specifically, has developed many of the practical skills I will be sharing.

I received my Master of Arts in Theology from Fuller Theological Seminary. While studying there I was taught more about what God had shown my mother that night—specifically details of His true nature and the nature of the relationship He wants to have with us and wants us to have with our children. These things will be shared in this book as we discuss the difference between what a relationship looks like when it is under Law versus under Grace.

Now I have my own children and am reaping the benefits of implementing everything I have learned. I look forward to the many more children I believe God will bless my husband and I with, and whom we can raise using these skills which make parenting a joy and a reward. Through the challenges presented by my own children I've learned much about the reality of Grace-Based Discipline. No, it's not easy, but nothing about parenting is. Just as with any task, when the work is put into doing it right the actual job becomes easier. As I lose sleep being awake with my toddler I am comforted to know I will not need to lose as much sleep when he becomes a teenager.

There is so much that I want to say on the subject of parenting; I only pray that God will show me what is to be in this book and what is to wait. I also pray that you will be blessed as you read. Some of what you read in this book may convict you; these are things that God is telling you to look at more closely. Other passages in this book, I hope, will encourage you. If, however, at any point you feel condemned put down the book and pray. Condemnation is not from God and it is not from me. It is from the enemy. He may be using old messages playing in your mind telling you how things should be done. Or, he may simply be telling you that you are a bad parent. Remember, he does not want you to be a good parent. Whatever you feel condemned about needs to be taken to God and He will show you what to do with it. I would recommend praying, each time before you pick up this book and each time that you put it down, that God will tell you what He would have you hear. Parenting is a vital role and an immense responsibility for anyone, but especially for a believer. The enemy would have us fail. This book is not divinely inspired Scripture, but it does come out of two generations of mothers spending years seeking God's heart. If you are seeking God's heart for your children, I trust that He will show you what you need to know for your family. I am grateful for any way in which He uses this book to do that.

Chapter Two
Law vs. Grace

Titus 2.3-5.

> **"Older women likewise are to be reverent in their behavior, not malicious gossips, nor enslaved to much wine, teaching what is good, that they may encourage the young women to love their husbands, to love their children, to be sensible, pure, workers at home, kind, being subject to their own husbands, that the word of God may not be dishonored."**[i]

I was shocked the day that I realized I was a Titus 2 woman. I always imagined Paul talking about old women—I mean <u>OLD</u> women. But he wasn't. The verse quoted above says "older" and refers to women who meet the qualification of being able to teach the things mentioned. I also am aware that I have two young children and not the several of varying ages that I would have had by this age in Biblical times. I am blessed because many older women whom I respect and to whom I have been highly accountable have mentored me. For those of you who may not have Titus women who you respect to teach you about mothering, I am sharing the things taught to me. With the industrialization of this country, and the creation of the nuclear family, many women find themselves with no older women to teach them. Also, thanks to the modern situation of so many women working outside the home, many of our generation were raised without a mother in the home to model parenting. So, where are women of our generation to look?

Just being older does not make a woman a Titus 2 woman. Titus 2 women are women who can teach the things called for in the above verses—how to love a husband and children and bring honor to the word of God. Unfortunately, many women of the previous few generations have been taught not by older women, but by the medical community or by parenting journals, many of which did not have Godly children as their end goal. These women do not have the right to teach the younger women as they do not meet the requirements of knowing the things required to be taught by this verse. Thankfully, I see that God is calling more and more Titus 2 women to step up and take their place in the teaching of Godly parenting in this day.

It is also interesting to me that most of the authors being touted as parenting experts today, especially in

Christian circles, are male. The Bible says nothing about men teaching women how to be mothers. Men have never been and will never be mothers. They need to be teaching men how to be men, how to be fathers, and how to support the role of the mother. While some men, like Dr. Sears, are teaching wonderful things as they write and teach with their wives, there are other men who have caused much damage attempting to teach women how to mother.

I also want to share something about the foundation of a teaching that has gained popularity in recent years and has been destroying many relationships between mothers and their children. It has also done much damage to the husband-wife relationship by encouraging parents to discount the intuition that God put into mothers in exchange for a behavioral model of parenting. I am not suggesting that all modern behaviorists would agree with this teaching, but behaviorism is the foundation of this teaching, despite the man's insistence that behaviorism is evil, and I wish to expose one example of what happens when men attempt to teach women how to parent babies and young children. There is also a claim that this teaching is supported by Scripture, but where it actually comes from is circa 1916, when the "most influential psychology of the day" was making itself felt.

> This was the "Behaviorism" of Professor John Broadus Watson of Johns Hopkins University. "Behaviorism" held

that the only sound approach to the study of the child was through its behavior. The basic contention was that only the objectively observable could constitute the data of science. What could not be observed—the child's wishes, needs, and feelings—were excluded from the behaviorist's interest and were therefore treated as if they did not exist. The behaviorists insisted upon treating children as if they were mechanical objects that could be wound up any which way one pleased; children were at the mercy of their environment, and parents could by their own behavior make them into anything they wished. Sentimentality was to be avoided, because any show of love or close physical contact made the child too dependent upon the affections of others. One must not spoil children with affection.[ii]

This teaching affected pediatricians and what they told the parents of their patients:

Pediatricians advised parents to maintain a sophisticated aloofness from their children, keeping them at arm's length, and managing them on a schedule characterized by both objectivity and regularity. They were to be fed by the clock, *not* on demand, and only at definite and regular times. If they cried during the intervals of three or four hours between feedings, they were to be allowed to do so until the clock announced the next feeding time. During such intervals of crying they were not to be picked up, since if one yielded to such weak impulses the child would be spoiled, and thereafter every time he desired something he would cry. And so millions of mothers sat and cried along with their babies, but, as genuinely loving mothers obedient to the best thinking on the subject, bravely resisted the "animal impulse" to pick them up and comfort them in their arms. Most mothers felt that this could not be right, but who were they to argue with the authorities? No one ever told them that an "authority" is one who *should* know.[iii]

If this teaching sounds familiar to you, please recognize that these are its roots and it is not God's way. It may come as a shock to find that this is not a new, or Biblically sanctioned, style of parenting. Unfortunately many parents who have truly desired to be Godly parents have been led astray by this teaching. If you are among them, please do not think it's too late. God can restore what the enemy has destroyed. What you will find in this book is God's heart for families—a discussion of the Biblical example for parenting which God, Himself, has modeled for us.

Dads Are Parents Too

As a woman, I do not believe it is my responsibility to teach fathers how to be fathers. Does this mean that there is no value for men in what I am sharing? No, I do not believe that is the case. What I believe is that

21

Scriptural wisdom is Scriptural wisdom, for men and women, regardless of whom is presenting it. For example, God designed a woman's body to breastfeed. Teaching that breastfeeding is best, or the scientific principals of breastfeeding, can be done by anyone. However, a woman should be responsible for teaching these womanly arts to the breastfeeding woman while a man needs to be responsible for teaching a man how to support his breastfeeding wife.

Historically, women were primarily responsible for parenting the very young child. Fathers took on a more active role around age 6—after child-led weaning. Fathers were especially responsible for preparing young boys for adulthood, and rights of passage usually occurred at puberty, which, in the Jewish community occurred at the age of 13. Our Western culture has changed life for a family dramatically from what it has been historically, and still is for non-Western cultures. Where a woman in the past had a community of women to help with the parenting of the young child, today she has herself and her husband, and perhaps one or more friends or relatives who happen to live close enough to provide occasional assistance. Because of this ever-increasing reliance on a husband to help in parenting the baby and young child, men's ideas on how to parent children of this age have become more pronounced and are often seen as the "expert" advice. However, it is the woman who has been designed and called by God to parent these young people and, while the help of a husband/father is vital in our culture today, the man would be wise to follow his wife's lead during these early years. Dr. William Sears provides an excellent resource for fathers in <u>On Becoming A Father</u> and acknowledges that a father must first understand the mother-infant bond before he can understand his role in parenting in the early years.[iv] It is by following the mother's cues in the early years that a father will provide the help and leadership at this important time and will create a bond with his children, which will be vital when the father takes on even more responsibility as a leader in providing discipline. It is also at this important time that a man's choices pave the future of his relationship with his wife.

Children grow up and move out of the house. The marriage relationship comes before the children and it must continue after the children have grown. While children are young it is time to be building a strong foundation for your marriage. The strongest foundations are not being built where there is arguing about parenting choices or if a woman is resenting her husband for pressuring her to ignore her God-given intuition. God created women to be the primary parent during the early years of a child's life. This is made clear from our Titus 2 verse and through an acknowledgement that, biologically, it is the woman who is designed to birth, nourish, and respond to the basic needs of a young child. For a man to accept and respect this call on his wife is for him to lift her to a place of honor. This can only strengthen the foundation of the marriage and the bond between husband and wife.

A Biblical Approach To Parenting

What does "a Biblical approach to parenting" mean? I am not presenting how *I* believe parents and children should behave while pulling scriptures from here and there to support my ideas. That is called prooftexting and is not the appropriate way of studying the Bible. If one verse is taken out of the Bible, studied alone and put back in, it corrupts everything around it. This is what has been done for years in the church when it comes to parenting. The idea of breaking the Bible down into its individual units was very popular in seminaries for a long time. The limitations of that approach to the Word of God have been recognized and most scholars now see the importance of looking at each scripture in light of what the entire Bible reveals. I am attempting to share what my study of Scripture has revealed to be the nature of God as parent. There is not a God of wrath who is revealed in the Old Testament, and a second God, a God of grace revealed in the New Testament. God is God, in both the Old and the New Testaments, and grace is present throughout the law. The law reveals God's standard and serves the purpose of showing that man, alone, can never live up to that standard. Even the law had built into it sacrifices so that when the law was violated, the relationship between man and God could be restored. It is clear throughout Scripture that God is very concerned with relationship. He desires relationship with us and we receive much instruction on how to conduct ourselves in our relationships with each other through reading his Word.

Sin

Since many Christian parenting philosophies are rooted in the idea that children are born with a sinful nature, I want to address the issue of original sin and the need for salvation. The word translated, "sin" is an archery term and means "missing the mark." It has to do with shooting an arrow towards a target and not hitting the bull's eye. The idea is that we are aiming towards the perfect plan God has for our lives and, on our own, we will miss the mark—or sin. Jesus explained that the law could be summed up in two concepts—love God and love your neighbor. In Romans Paul goes further to explain that if what you're doing doesn't offend God then you're fine—unless what you're doing offends another believer. Offending that believer offends God and you need to rethink your actions. It's that simple. If you strive to fulfill these two ideals, loving God and loving your neighbor, you will hit the mark; of course you can only accomplish these things with God's help.

God told Adam not to eat from the fruit of the Tree of the Knowledge of Good and Evil. Adam didn't obey; he sinned. When Adam sinned he damaged the relationship he had with God. He gained the thought processes to determine for himself what was good and what was evil rather than relying on what God said was good and evil. The entire philosophical discussion of situational ethics is an attempt for each person to be given room for their own determination of what is good and what is evil. The obvious problems occur when there is disagreement between what two people consider "good" or "evil." Genesis teaches us that it's much clearer than that. Any time man chooses for himself what is good and doesn't rely on God's teaching then he sins—or misses the mark.

Because of Adam's original sin, every person is now born with this ability, and inclination, to choose for himself what is good. However, making a choice requires skills that are not developed in young children and often, young children make unwise choices. A Jewish child becomes an adult at 13—even if this isn't the "age of accountability" I think it's a good example to follow and a target age to shoot for in our parenting. By this age a child should be able to make a responsible and Godly decision. Up until this age, and after it, it is our responsibility as parents to teach, through instruction and modeling, who God is, how to have a relationship with Him, and what He would have us choose in different situations. I believe we teach this best by following God's example for us. He got down on our level, was born as a man, and taught us while He modeled for us how to behave. He loved us and sacrificed himself for us. He became a servant for us. He warned us about natural consequences and, when they are not too dangerous, allows us to experience them. Ultimately, He died so that we don't have to.[v]

It's not that any of us did anything "so wrong that we need salvation." It's that God has set a standard and we have a choice—live up to the standard in our own ability or enter into relationship with Jesus Christ and not be held accountable for everywhere we fall short just because we are human. The fact is, on our own, and even with His help, we miss the mark. It happens every day in a variety of different ways. Every time we have a selfish thought we have fallen short of what God would have for our lives. As Jesus explained, if we are angry with our brother we are as guilty of breaking God's law as if we had killed the person.[vi] Salvation is God's means of distributing Grace to us so that we aren't held accountable for all the ways we fall short. One of the main points throughout the Old Testament is that even when men have God's Law they can't live up to it on their own. With salvation we can have the relationship Adam had with God before he sinned. This is why the message Jesus taught was called the "Gospel," or "Good News." Unfortunately, what is taught at a lot of churches isn't very good news—especially for children.

As parents we are called to follow the examples of God and of Jesus and relate to and understand our children. We are called to teach and model Godly living and decision-making. We are called to warn about natural consequences and shield our children from those they're not ready for while holding ourselves back and letting them experience those they are ready for and need. In order to do any of this we must learn what is age-appropriate. We are called to serve our children by putting their needs ahead of our own comforts. This does not mean that we should give them everything they want. It does mean that we make choices for their best interests ahead of our comfort (breastfeeding on demand; being up with a sick child or one who just can't sleep; striving to find the underlying cause of poor behavior instead of beating it out of a child). The practices of attachment parenting not only create a strong foundation for the parent-child relationship, they encourage this sacrifice on behalf of a parent for their child. Ultimately we are called to sacrifice ourselves for our children. These are things most Christians are challenged to do for their fellow Christian, but rarely is it applied to parenting. The verse that is translated "Train up a child in the way he should go, even when he is old he will not depart from it"[vii] is also archery language. Archers would fashion their own arrows and each one was unique, with its own bent—like children. It was the archer's responsibility to know the bent of his arrows well enough that he could adjust his shot so they would fly straight and hit the mark. We need to know our children so well that we see God's unique design in them and work with them the way they need so that when we shoot them out into the world they fly straight and hit the mark God has for them. The process of getting to know our children needs to start at birth.

Our children are not evil, but they are destined to choose their own way over God's unless we teach them otherwise. I want to model God's love and grace for my children, while still holding them to a high standard.

This is what God does for us and I want them to eventually have this type of relationship with God.

Two Kinds Of Relationships

What are some of the major differences between life under the Law and life under Grace?

Major difference number one: Security in relationship to God. Even though the Law had sacrifices built into it as a means of Grace, the sacrifices required death as atonement for sins and the sacrifices were performed for each sin. One's relationship with God was never secure, but was dependent on the performance of the proper sacrifice. Under Grace, Jesus was our one-time ultimate sacrifice. He died once and for all to forgive us our sins if only we believe in Him. Once we allow Jesus' death to be the atoning sacrifice for our sins we are welcomed into the family of God as His children and we never again have to fear a loss of the status of sons and daughters of the King.

Major difference number two: Ability to fulfill requirements of the Law. It is a misconception to think that under Grace we are not expected to observe the Law. The Law is unchanging as God's revelation to man of how we can please Him. "All Scripture is inspired by God and profitable for teaching, for reproof, for correction, for training in righteousness; that the man of God may be adequately equipped for every good work."[viii] Paul is referring to the Torah, the books of the Law, as the Bible as we know it had not yet been compiled. Under Grace we receive the Holy Spirit. Through His indwelling and empowering us we are able to fulfill the requirements of the Law and when we fall short it is not counted against us. Without Grace and the indwelling power of the Holy Spirit, we are destined to repeatedly fail. That is why under the Law there was the need for repeated sacrifices. Man, left to his own, will fail miserably at keeping the Law. Thank God He has a better plan.

Major difference number three: Relationship to others. The Torah, or the Law, was seen by the Israelites as a way to keep them separated from other cultures and communities. They were to be set apart in their beliefs and their actions and this kept them from developing relationships with non-Israelites. Others could accept the Law and be welcomed into the Israelite community, but they must then be set apart as well. Under Grace we receive the ability and the admonition to be in the world but not of it. It is the Holy Spirit within us that separates us and keeps us holy. We are to be separate and set-apart in our beliefs and actions, but not elite in our relationships with others. It is through relationship with believers that non-believers are exposed to the teachings of Jesus. The Great Commission was given that we should "Go therefore and make disciples of all the nations, baptizing them in the name of the Father and the Son and the Holy Spirit, teaching them to observe all that I commanded you."[ix] We must lay down our lives and pick up our cross daily. Believers are called to sacrifice for and to serve others.

What do these differences between law and grace mean to parenting? Parents who parent under a system of law establish relationships with their children based upon a set of requirements the child must meet in order to have a relationship with the parent. When a law is violated, atonement must be made and a sacrifice must be made in the form of a punishment to the child. Only after the proper administration of a punishment can relationship be reestablished with the parent. Until that happens, the relationship between parent and child is strained and, in the child's mind, in question. There is a clear separation between the parent as the one laying down the law and the child as the one held accountable to the law. Rather than modeling servanthood and sacrifice, these parents simply require it of the children. Elitism can also develop between parents using this approach and parents choosing other methods of parenting.

I am amazed that parents would choose to raise their children under an environment of law when the Law does not address issues of parenting except to say:

> If any man has a stubborn and rebellious son who will not obey his father or his mother, and when they chastise him, he will not even listen to them, then his father and mother shall seize him, and bring him out to the elders of his city at the gateway of his hometown. And they shall say to the elders of his city, "This son of

ours is stubborn and rebellious, he will not obey us, he is a glutton and a drunkard." Then all the men of his city shall stone him to death; so you shall remove the evil from your midst, and all Israel shall hear of it and fear.[x]

In reality, there is no recorded event of this ever happening. The point, as the Rabbis understood it, was to emphasize the importance of raising your child to be a responsible adult. Also, please note that the child had to be old enough to be a glutton and a drunkard. This is not a verse dealing with young children.

So, if the Law is silent about how to raise our children, except to say that we must do so and we must do so responsibly, what does the New Testament tell us? The New Testament is just as silent in regards to parenting styles and practices. So how does one develop a Biblical parenting style? I'll tell you. We develop a parenting style based on Grace. We look to Jesus so that we may follow His example. "Christian" means "follower of Christ." Christ is revealed through Scripture and the way we are to conduct our lives is made known to us. These principles apply to how we are to Love the Lord our God with all our hearts, minds, and souls, and love our neighbors as ourselves.[xi] Through this the entire Law and the prophets will be fulfilled. Let's take a look at how we are to love our children.

Chapter Three
Boundaries

I am not going to teach you how to change your children so that they will be better children. I am going to talk with you about changing yourselves so that you are better parents to the children God gave you.

You won't hear this discussed in many circles today, but more people are coming to realize that punishment doesn't work. It may cause a child to comply out of fear, but what happens when the child gets too big to be afraid of you? What if the child decides to stop complying despite the fear? What do you do? Hit harder? Hit more? Longer time-outs? What do you do?

Most parent-child relationships look like a tug-of-war game with the parent on one end of the rope and the child on the other. The rope is the child's will. Both parent and child are battling for control of the child's will and this is destined to result in a power struggle. If you are your child's opponent you can expect them to not listen to you and to see your attempts to control them in a negative light. God desires our willing obedience; I do not want less from my children. How can I require more of my children than God requires of me? Forced obedience has lost its value. The only way to win this tug-of-war with your child is to recognize that it takes two people to be in a power struggle and drop your end of the rope. After you let go of your child's will, get out of their face and move yourself so that you're standing beside them and looking down life's road with them. It is from this strategic position that you will be able to help guide your child in the choices they make about their wills and their lives. Instead of the battle other "experts" try to tell you how to win, I want to help you be on the same team as your child. Instead of their opponent you can be their captain.

Family Leadership

Leadership. Everyone seems to be talking about leadership these days. It's very important in the business world. This is because the business world has finally realized that leadership is not the same as management. Management is the ability to get the day-to-day things done. It is important, but not as important as leadership. Leadership is the ability to see and set a goal and then take a group toward that desired goal. The two things I consider the most important as I have studied leadership are: 1) you lead out of who you are (character); and 2) you lead by example (modeling). I find it especially interesting that in sign language the sign for management is made with both hands, fists closed and in front of you alternating back and forth, as if you were pulling on reigns. I believe it symbolizes of the tug-of-war that exists when someone with a management style is trying to get someone else to do something the second person does not want to do and for which they see no importance. The sign for leadership, however, looks very much like a mother cradling a baby. More and more the idea of "mother and child" is being used as a model for leadership.[xii]

How does one lead a family? Steven Covey, in his widely acclaimed book *Seven Habits of Highly Successful People*[xiii], talks about starting with the end in mind. The idea of starting with the end in mind is, essentially, to have an idea of where you are going before you start. Then, keep that idea in mind as you go and make sure that each decision you make gets you closer to your desired destination.

The first step in leading your family is to decide where you want to go. My husband and I have discussed many ideas about where we want to go and some things we know for sure about our desired destination. We desire to put God first in our lives and at the center of everything we do. The first question we try to ask when making a decision is, "Would this please the Lord?" It is very popular today for young people to wear jewelry with the letters "WWJD?" on them. This stands for "What would Jesus do?" I know of many young people who wear this jewelry and do not know how to answer the question. They do not have a relationship with Jesus so they do not know what He would do. I feel that our question is more to the point for those of us who do have a relationship with Jesus. How do you answer the question? I would recommend that you set your first priority as pleasing God, and then set goals that please Him.

We want to have a large family and to make family a priority. Since the first command in the Bible is "Be fruitful and multiply . . .."[xiv] I believe this is something that would please the Lord. The Bible makes it clear that children are a blessing from the Lord and we do not want to limit the blessings that God may choose to give us. Having a large family is one of our priorities. Whether you want a small family or a large one, you are parents because you have at least one blessing from the Lord. I would challenge you to pray about how many blessings you are open to God giving you.

We desire to raise our children in the love of the Lord. What does this mean to us? This means that every time we do something we must ask ourselves if it is modeling a Christ-like behavior for any child who may be watching. Children learn from what you do more than what you say. You can tell a child to pray until you are blue in the face but unless that child sees you pray you can pretty much forget about them doing it. This means modeling a love for God as well as a love for each other. It means asking what we have done to care for the widow, the orphan, and the stranger—the least of these. This also means loving our children unconditionally the way God loves us. The way our children perceive us is how they will understand God. If we are judgmental and punishing, they will see God as judgmental and punishing. If we withhold our love when our children do something that doesn't please us, they will see God as withholding His love and they will fear losing their salvation. If you have either of these views of God yourself I encourage you to read His Word and see that He is a God who loves us sacrificially and unconditionally and "when we are faithless, He remains faithful; for He cannot deny Himself."[xv]

I do not believe a parent can teach a child love, joy, peace, patience, kindness, goodness, gentleness or self-control. If these are the fruits of the Spirit[xvi] then they come from being rooted in the Lord and it is the Spirit that produces them. I can teach my child to sit quietly and wait without complaining, and this is a social skill my child would benefit from in this culture, but I am not teaching him patience. Patience is a sacrificial waiting that comes out of love for another and a desire to not rush them. How can I teach this? How many of us, as adults, even have this fruit growing in abundance in our lives? But I can teach my child how to be rooted in the Lord. I can desire the growth of these Spiritual fruit in my life so that my child can see these things modeled for him and desire them for himself.

Here is the list of five goals my husband and I have in parenting our children:

1. In all things, do what is pleasing to the Lord.

2. Be fruitful and multiply.

3. Raise our children in the love of the Lord.

4. Have Spiritual fruit growing in our own lives.

5. Teach our children how to be rooted in God.

These are five somewhat lofty goals. We are not foolish enough to think that we can accomplish any of these perfectly, but these are our targets. When a situation arises which requires us to make a decision about what to do, we can ask ourselves if what we want to do will help us accomplish these goals or contradict them. What goals do you have for your family? What road would God have you walk? Where will your boundaries from God be narrow and where is the road broad for you? At the end of this chapter there are some pages specifically set up to help you create your own family goals.

Leadership comes into play as you pray about and set your family's goals, and as you keep your family on track for achieving them. Remember, however, that the goals cannot be what you want someone else to do. They must be things you actually have control over. For example, we can have as a goal to teach our children how to be rooted in the Lord, because we can teach them. We cannot have as a goal that our children will be rooted in the Lord. This is a decision each person must make for himself and we cannot control that decision any more than the Lord does. If God gives us free will to choose Him, how can we do any less with our children? I do not want a rebellious child. But I would rather have a child who is openly rebellious to God so that I can pray for them and continue to model God's love for them, than have a child who is pretending to love the Lord while sinning in his heart. How will I know what to pray for this child? In working towards my goal of modeling God to my children, I want to teach them honesty in all things and in all relationships, especially in their relationship to God.

We have also devised a family motto to which we will be taking every decision we have to make—from how to react to something to whether or not something should be done.

"Life's about relationships and we get things done along the way."

Some people get caught up in conflict about what should be done or how it should be done. I was recently told the story (by one of the people involved) that a husband told his wife what to do and she responded that she didn't like how he had spoken to her. She felt he was being bossy and disrespectful. She would have preferred that he tell her he would like it done, or, at least, ask her to do it. He thought this sounded like a waste of words and all he wanted was to get the job done. I commented that getting things done is important (sometimes) but how we say things and the attitude with which we communicate is relationship. My husband and I discussed this incident and looked at how we sometimes communicate with the question, "Are we worried about getting things done or are we putting forth the effort to work on our relationship?" With this motto we are stating that we are about relationship.

I believe that God is about relationship. The books of the law are about how to be holy as God is holy[xvii]. In the Garden of Eden God walked with Adam and Eve and had communion with them and they knew first hand what God wanted from them—He showed and told them. The books of the Law were necessary for the Hebrews because they had lost relationship with God and He had not been modeling it for them. Jesus came to Earth and died on the cross to bridge the gap created by sin so that fellowship could be restored between mankind and God. We have Christ's life to look to when deciding what to do. We have a restored relationship with God. It was God who initiated that restoration, not man.[xviii] Jesus goes so far as to say that if you are offering a sacrifice and remember that your brother has something against you, you are to leave your sacrifice at the altar and go to your brother and be reconciled to him.[xix] God is about relationships. As we go through life together in relationship, things get done.

Relationships

Relationships take time, effort, communication, and conflict resolution to succeed. Anyone who thinks that a relationship should be easy has never been in one. Let's look at the different relationships that exist within a family, specifically at the husband/wife relationship and then at the parent/child relationship.

We start with a man and a woman. "And God created man in His own image, in the image of God He created him; male and female He created them."[xx] And the man and the woman were equal—sharing dominion over God's creation. They were helpmates. And they became husband and wife. Husband and wife are enhancements of the roles of man and woman. The husband has not ceased to be a man and the wife has not ceased to be a woman. Instead, the husband is a man with a specific role—specific privileges and responsibilities; and the wife is a woman with a specific role—specific privileges and responsibilities. A wife can never stop being a wife and a husband can never stop being a husband. Even after death or divorce, the man and woman will still have been husband and wife and will retain the influence of that experience. A divorced couple is referred to as ex-husband and ex-wife, not as simply man and woman. When one mate dies we are left with a widow or a widower. In both of these instances, they have not moved backwards to being only man and woman, but have again enhanced their role to include man and woman, husband and wife, and the next role. There is no going backwards in life.

In the same way, becoming a father or mother is a moving forward to an enhanced role. The man and woman become husband and wife and then father and mother. Once a father, a man can never go back to being only a husband. The man will always be a father. Once a mother, the woman can never go back to being only a wife. She will always be a mother. There is, and has been for quite some time, a great push for fathers and mothers to take time to be only husband and wife and to put their husband/wife relationship as a priority. This is a futile attempt to go backwards. Since they can never go back to before they were parents, fathers and mothers can have special time alone, but they will never cease to be fathers and mothers. Even when children grow and leave home, or if they die, the father and mother will still be a father and mother. How do these relationships work? Let's start with what happens when a man and woman become husband and wife. The ceremony is exciting. A day neither will ever forget. It's an event marking the forever passage into a new relationship for the couple. And then the work begins. The first couple of years are spent getting to know each other's habits and rules. How does she fold the towels? When does he like to shower? What direction does the toilet paper go on the roll? During this getting-to-know-you time there will be conflict. This is inevitable. Any couple that tells you they don't have conflict is either not getting to know each other or is lying.

There are many skills that can be learned for dealing with conflict. There is great dysfunction in a relationship where one partner gets their way all the time and the other partner never gets their way. When there is a need for either person, it needs to be met. In conflict, sometimes there will have to be compromise—

where each person gives a little to get a little. This is not the ideal solution, however, because in compromise each partner wins, but each partner also loses. The ideal end to a conflict is found in resolving the conflict. Resolution occurs when partners approach the problem together seeking a solution that will be best for everyone. Neither partner approaches the problem with a predetermined solution that they are defending. They come together to the problem and seek the best answer for their marriage. And every couple will come to their own, different, solution that works best for them. Conflict resolution can be used in making decisions about who will handle the finances, where the couple will live, will they buy or rent, and whose family to visit for the holidays. Obviously, there is no right or wrong answer to any of these situations and the solutions for each couple will vary. Each couple must determine what works best for them.

And just when you think you have everything resolved and you are in agreement about how things need to run in your family, along comes a new member who must be included in the relationship dynamics. First, the husband and wife enhance their roles to become mother and father. As discussed above, father includes husband and man and mother includes wife and woman. But the roles of father and mother have additional privileges and responsibilities. Second, also as discussed above, any relationship where one person is always getting their way and the other person is never getting their way is a dysfunctional relationship. This includes families where the father or mother is always getting their way, and the child's needs and wishes are not considered. Third, resolution is still the ideal for solving a problem. In this new relationship, the baby will have many immediate needs that must be met. The practice of resolving is to be used to determine how to meet the needs of father, mother, and baby with the greatest amount of comfort for all involved and for the ultimate advancement of the family. Fourth, the resolutions achieved for each family will be different. This is why it is dangerous for any "teacher" or "child expert" to attempt to tell you how to raise your child. Your family's needs may not be unique, but your family is and how you approach meeting your needs will reflect your uniqueness and your goals as a family. I do want to make it perfectly clear at this point that I am talking about finding ways to meet everyone's needs, not deciding whose needs will be met.

For example, you all need sleep at night. Do you put your child in her own room and go in to her when she awakens? Put her in a crib or bassinet in your room and go to her when she wakes? Put her in bed with you so that you can meet her nighttime needs without waking up completely? The answer will be different for each family determined by the age of the child, the ability of each member of the family to sleep in each situation, and taking into consideration that a baby left to cry is suffering biological damage that can have long-term negative effects. Some parents prefer to have their baby in another room because mom or dad snores loudly and baby will be awake all night if in the same room. Some parents want their baby in the same room but are more comfortable with the baby in her own crib or bassinet. Some parents prefer to have their child in bed with them.

Under most circumstances people believe that to offer advice can be dangerous. Unfortunately, when it comes to parenting, everyone believes that they are an expert and believes that what worked for them will work for you. This is not always the case. Their family is not your family and their child is not your child. Conflict resolution is where no one comes to the discussion table with a predetermined solution to the problem. Instead, all parties involved (father, mother, and baby) are considered and a solution is sought that will benefit everyone. There may even need to be new solutions sought with each addition to your family.

Normal vs. Normative

Let us now discuss the difference between what is *Normal* and what is *Normative*. What is Normal, for this discussion, is the way God intended something to be. God is a God of order and design and, as Paul pointed out at the Areopagus, He has put His design into nature as a sign that He is and who He is.[xxi] What is Normative is what a culture prescribes as the norm. In every culture at every time there are different things that are culturally mandated as the norm, whether they are the way God intended them to be or not.

I understand that this may be a different use of the word *normal* than many are used to. Too often I hear, "My child is doing _____. Is this normal?" The truth is, yes, that is normal for that child. What each child does at any age is normal for that baby at that age. It's what God designed them to be able to do at that time. This is especially important when dealing with infants. It is normal for infants to cry and their wants are their needs. This is normal. This is the way God created infants to be. When dealing with normative, we are dealing with cultural preferences. The Bible was not written about people living in 19th-century Victorian England, although when many Christians talk about getting back to "traditional family values," this is the historical time to which they are referring. The Biblical cultures (for there were several) had different normative practices for parenting. However, the ideas of formula feeding, separate rooms for children, and scheduling are unique to the Western Culture within the last hundred years. No one should feel pressured to abide by any of these practices under the belief that they are God's ideal.

In addition to the need being met what must always be considered in conflict resolution is the effect the solution will have on each member of the family. I mentioned above that allowing a child to cry unattended has a negative biological effect. The more research that is done in this area, the more dangerous it is seen to be.[xxii] There is also the emotional danger of allowing a child to cry. Let me ask this question: How would you feel if, in your first year of marriage, you became devastated for some reason and through your tears attempted to communicate this pain and your need for comfort to your spouse? What if your spouse responded by turning to you and saying, "I really am not in the mood to deal with this. You need to go in the bedroom and cry alone. I'll come in to check on you in twenty minutes, but I'm sure you'll feel better by then anyway." Would you trust your spouse in the future? Would you feel comfortable going into the bedroom to cry alone for twenty minutes and return feeling better? Would you feel safe in your marriage? Would you question if you had made a wise decision marrying this person? Would you attempt to share your pain with them in the future? I believe that most of us would feel horribly betrayed and abandoned. I know that with my husband, even if he can't fix the problem, I feel better if he just holds me until I'm done crying.

Babies have no way to communicate except through crying. When they are crying they are letting their parents know, in the only way they can, that they have a need that must be met. The parent may not understand the need. The parent may think the need is silly by adult standards. But children are little people, not little adults. When left to cry alone they are given the very clear message that there is no one to meet their needs and that they are not worthy of having needs. If this technique is successful in the child not continuing to cry it is because at this very young age one of their first lessons in this life has been that they do not count and their needs will not be met. Often these babies enter into infant depression and show signs of failure to thrive[xxiii]. When done to the extreme, this is child neglect and the parents can be prosecuted for the abuse they are inflicting on their child. There is nothing loving or godly about conveying this message to a baby.

Children need to learn that they are not the center of the universe, but that is a lesson for a later time when the child can comprehend these things. And, let's be honest, how many adults have really learned this lesson? It took mankind thousands of years until Galileo to learn that the Earth and man are not at the center of the universe. Is there really any rush to teach this to our infants? Every child learns their place in the family as they grow and learn to relate to the other family members. The youngest child learns that the older children will not always turn over their toys just because they demand them. Children learn they will not always get what they want at the store when mom and dad don't buy it for them. Children learn all of these important things when it is an age appropriate lesson.

During the first year of life there is no justification for letting a child cry without responding and there is no age appropriate lesson being taught to that child. Even if you can't fix the problem, it is a much healthier lesson that you are teaching your child if you hold them until they feel better. This will teach them that life is safe and mommy and daddy can be trusted. Had the spouse in the earlier example responded in a more loving and attentive way I believe that the grieving spouse would have felt affirmed and validated and would be willing to openly communicate with them in the future. This is the lesson a child must learn if the parents want communication later in the child's life. There will come a time in the life of every parent who lets their child cry it out when they wonder why their child does not come to them. The answer is, they learned well not to.

Watch any daytime talk show and eventually you will see a parent who is angry over their child's behavior and the child's complaint is always, "My parent(s) don't listen to me." Listen to your children. You may not understand them, but eventually you will. You may not like what you hear, but you can do your job of parenting better if you listen. This starts with the infant. During the first couple of years of your child's life, you are laying a foundation. They may not remember being left to cry, or whether you responded every time they cried, but they will know whether it feels safe to share with you. They will know whether they feel that they are valued and worthy of having feelings. The child who feels valued and worthy and who feels safe communicating with their parents will be less likely to become involved in drugs, gangs, adolescent sex, or any other activity that children engage in to feel loved and accepted. Your child will know they are loved by you and will not have to seek that love from others.[xxiv]

Take some time to think about what you've read in this chapter and then use this space to create your own family motto. I've asked some questions to get you started and given you some space to work out your answers.

Your Family Goals and a Family Motto:

What areas do you feel God speaking about in your life?

Are there things you believe He's specifically called you to do?

What values are the most important to you and your family?

What do you want your children to learn before they become adults?

Our Family Goals:

_____

_____

_____

_____

Now, based on your goals and what you've determined is important to you, try to come up with a family motto that will reflect those goals. Remember that your goals and motto may change as your family grows, but it's a good idea to have a place to start.

Our Family Motto:

"_____

_____
_____ "

Chapter Four
What About The Rod?

Is there a place for punishment in Christian parenting? NO. Why? IT DOESN'T WORK. People learn 20% from what is spoken and 80% from what is not spoken. If I tell you I love you while I hit you—what message is louder? If I tell you I love you while I lead you to time-out/isolation—what message is louder? Worse still, what if I spank you while I yell at you for being horrible? Punishment may stop behavior in the here and now but in the long run, it will not produce the desired results. Some children even have an immediate poor reaction to negative attention from their parent. Punishment creates the illusion of a lesson learned by demanding results while Grace-Based Discipline teaches the lessons and trusts that when they are learned the results will be present.

"Discipline" means "to teach," "to educate," "to disciple." "Chastise" means "to correct" and is usually understood to be a verbal correction. Our children need to be taught and educated in right behavior and corrected from wrong behavior. The Bible never tells us to do this cruelly or painfully.

At this point most people will ask, "Doesn't Proverbs say we have to spank?" No. First of all, the genre of Proverbs is one of Wisdom sayings, not Law. So, even if one or more of the Proverbs did say that it was wisdom to spank, that doesn't mean that everyone has to do so. But Proverbs doesn't say that it is wisdom to spank. "Do not hold back discipline from the child, although you beat him with the rod, he will not die."[xxv] Doesn't this even suggest it should be painful? If this Scripture were talking about literally hitting a child with a stick it would be lying. The truth is, you can kill a child by hitting them—with or without a stick. So the meaning of the verse becomes clear only through approaching it in the context of the Scriptures as a whole and an understanding of the rod.

There are ten different words in Scripture that are translated to "rod" in English.[xxvi] The one used in verses that are most often cited to endorse spanking is "shebet," or the rod of authority. There are three rods of authority in Scripture. A shepherd's stick, a walking stick, or a king's scepter. These sticks were not instruments for hitting the one under the holder's authority (while I'm not saying they never were used that way, it would not be the idea being conveyed by referring to them). For example, a shepherd might use his staff to kill a lion that was threatening his sheep, but he would not beat his sheep with it. A walking stick might be used to fend off an attacker (animal or human) but was not intended for beating those under the care of the one using it. We see from the example of Esther that when she entered the King's presence it was when he held out his scepter to her that she was welcomed to him and granted permission to speak. It is when the rod was withheld (spared) that death fell on the person who dared enter the King's presence.[xxvii]

All three rods were symbols of the authority held by the man to whom they belonged. If the man took the responsibilities represented by his rod seriously he would use that authority to do his job. This means, among other things, that a man would raise his children using his authority. If he were to spare, or withhold, his rod and not raise his children using his authority he would have spoiled children. Correction should not be withheld from a child. A child won't die from being corrected. "Although you beat him..." this is the same "beat" as when the sun beat down on Jonah and is referring to a steady presence. A child will not die from constant correction and discipline. I read this scripture as support for my husband and I to be constantly responsible for training our children and using whatever methods of discipline we use in a constant and consistent manner for the sake of our child's eternal soul.

Now, even if you do believe that this verse is talking about spanking, let me point out some things:

1) In the day that it was written, men were responsible for the discipline of a child after a certain age—and then only the male children. Women were primarily responsible for the care of the infants and young children until the boys' training was turned over to the men. As this is advice from a father to his son on how to discipline, I do not believe that it need be applied to mothers or the discipline of young children. The Biblical instruction for women is given in Titus 2 where we learn only that a woman is to love her children.

2) Proverbs is a book of wisdom sayings, not a book of Law. The only scripture in the Law books that addresses discipline is this:

> "If any man has a stubborn and rebellious son who will not obey his father or his mother, and when they chastise him, he will not even listen to them, then his father and mother shall seize him, and bring him out to the elders of his city at the gateway of his home town. And they shall say to the elders of his city, 'This son of ours is stubborn and rebellious, he will not obey us, he is a glutton and a drunkard.' Then all of the men of his city shall stone him to death; so you shall remove the evil from your midst, and all Israel shall hear of it and fear."[xxviii]

The Biblical mandate for punishment of a rebellious son is stoning to death at the gateway of his hometown. Other than there being no recorded event of this ever happening, the "child" must be a stubborn, rebellious, disobedient, drunkard and glutton. This is not a small child—certainly not a toddler. The rabbis understand this verse to be conveying the seriousness with which God looks at a parent's responsibility to properly raise their children. This is the consequence for laying aside your rod of authority and not properly raising your child. Of course, I have never heard anyone who supports spanking also say that stoning your child to death is a valid choice if they are rebellious. But that's what God says. King Solomon said the things about the rod. I believe that if God wanted us to spank, He would have specifically addressed the issue in the books of the Law where He laid down what pleased Him. But He remained silent on hitting children. Could it be that this was one of the first lessons of Grace God wanted us to learn? Could it be that God had Grace-Based Discipline in mind even then? I believe so.

Now that we've dealt with the rod issue, let me suggest another approach to parenting:

Then Peter came and said to Him, "Lord, how often shall my brother sin against me and I forgive him? Up to seven times?"

Jesus said to him, "I do not say to you, up to seven times, but up to seventy times seven. For this reason the kingdom of heaven may be compared to a certain king who wished to settle accounts with his slaves. And when he had begun to settle them, there was brought to him one who owed him ten thousand talents. But since he did not have the means to repay, his lord commanded him to be sold, along with his wife and children and all that he had, and repayment to be made. The slave therefore falling down, prostrated himself before him, saying 'Have patience with me, and I will repay you everything.' And the lord of that slave felt compassion and released him and forgave him the debt.

"But that slave went out and found one of his fellow slaves who owed him a hundred denarii; and he seized him and began to choke him, saying, 'Pay back what you owe.' So his fellow slave fell down and began to entreat him, saying, 'Have patience with me and I will repay you.' He was unwilling however, but went and threw him in prison until he should pay back what was owed. So when his fellow slaves saw what had happened, they were deeply grieved and came and reposted to their lord all that had happened.

"Then summoning him, his lord said to him, 'You wicked slave, I forgave you all that debt because you entreated me. Should you not also have had mercy on your fellow slave, even as I had mercy on you?' And his lord, moved with anger, handed him over to the torturers until he should repay all that was owed him.

"So shall My heavenly Father also do to you, if each of you does not forgive his brother from your heart."[xxix]

No doubt we have all heard this passage of Scripture applied to us forgiving our brothers and sisters in Christ. I am not challenging that teaching.

What I would like to do is expand upon it. How many times have you heard this passage of Scripture applied to the parent-child relationship? I never have. But the application holds up. If we have been forgiven our sins against God, who are we to hold our children accountable to punishment for much more minor sins against us? Especially when our children's "sins" against us are usually something like not coming when we call them or flexing their two-year-old independence by telling us "no."

I read the Bible and ask how it applies to different areas of my life. I'm sure we've all heard preachers give sermons about New Testament passages and how they apply to our "brother"—-meaning the fellow Christian—or even to non-Christians. I would recommend that you read through the New Testament and ask how you can apply its teachings to your spouse and your children.

Also, the Bible speaks to the reader and calls you to obedience to its lessons. You, the reader. Not the person next to you. Not your co-worker. Not your spouse. Not your child. These are people who you cannot control. It speaks to you. What does this mean? "Children, obey your parents in the Lord, for this is right. HONOR YOUR FATHER AND MOTHER (which is the first commandment with a promise), THAT IT MAY BE WELL WITH YOU, AND THAT YOU MAY LIVE LONG ON THE EARTH."[xxx] Please note that the verse is speaking to the child—not to someone else who is expected to make the child obey.

Are you a child? We all are. Then honor your father and your mother. Let me also point out that the obedience called for in this verse is to the commandment to honor your father and your mother—not to any command given by the parent. This verse is often used to justify forcing children to be obedient to their parents. That is not the meaning or the intent of the words.

"And, fathers, do not provoke your children to anger; but bring them up in the discipline and instruction of the Lord."[xxxi] Are you a parent (a father, specifically, but a parent in general)? Then do not provoke your children to anger. I assure you that children feel anger at being hit or punished in any way. They may not express it. They may not be allowed to express it. But they feel anger. Instead, bring them up in the discipline and instruction of the Lord.

This example is also good for discussing something Paul often does in explaining relationships involving authority. He speaks to both parties in the relationship and calls them both into accountability for acknowledging God-given authority. In this relationship, it is the father who has the authority. The child is expected to honor that authority and the father expected to not abuse it. Because I am confident in my authority I can say that I am the mommy and what I say will happen. At the same time, I can turn my concern to how we all feel about each other in the relationship.

Chapter Five
The Tools

There are essentially three styles of discipline: permissive, authoritarian, and Grace-Based Discipline (GBD).[xxxii] I have heard many good descriptions of these three styles of parenting, but I would like to offer my own. Imagine a field for as far as the eye can see, and a path running through it. The permissive parent would allow their child to go anywhere—on the path, through the field, out of sight—and to do anything while they were there. The authoritarian parent is the one who takes the little feet stickers that are found in "How to Dance" manuals and puts them on the path while insisting that their child step only on the feet as they have been laid out. The GBD parent insists that their child stay on the path, but allows them to choose where to step and how fast to travel on it.

The permissive style is obviously dangerous. The child is allowed to go anywhere and do anything he chooses while lacking the experience to make wise choices. Assuming that the path leads somewhere important (like adulthood) it is important that the child follow the path. The permissive child may or may not follow the path. Often, sitting by the duck pond is much more enjoyable than walking. But children must all get to adulthood eventually. The permissively parented child will not have a healthy respect for boundaries because none were placed on them growing up. They might take long lunch hours because they had to go to that restaurant regardless of the wait and they might be in poor physical health because watching your diet and exercise are not fun. They are often unable to see how their choices affect others. They are so used to getting their way that when they do not they may have difficulty handling it.

The child raised by authoritarian parents might have different problems. They follow the path to adulthood, but they are not allowed to enjoy it. They develop responsibility, but they often do not develop emotionally. No one was concerned with validating their feelings on the path, so they may not be very in touch with them when they reach adulthood. These are the adults who can be by the book and not consider other people's feelings. Children of authoritarian parents often struggle with rebellion as they near the end of the path—adolescence. Children must separate from their parents and become adults at some point in their development. They will either begin to separate between the ages of 18 months to three years (often called the terrible twos because children learn that they can say "no" and have their own opinion) or they have to do all of the separation during adolescence. One way or another it will be done by the time they reach 18 or the child will not be able to function as an adult. Authoritarian parents are so hung up on having things their way that they do not allow their toddlers to begin the separation from their parents. This style of parenting is also called punitive parenting because it relies primarily on punishment to enforce the rules. "No" is a word only used by mom and dad—and used too often. Children are not allowed to express any opinion that differs from mom and dad and they learn that they are not valuable as individuals. These children still need to separate before age 18. All of their separation will have to occur in their teenage years when they are able to be out of their parents' reach and they will be more likely to act out in inappropriate ways because they do not have a well-developed self-image.

Then there are the children raised by GBD parents. This style of parenting is the one modeled by God as He parents believers. This is the style of parenting that takes into consideration all of the members of the family and their behavior as well as their feelings and needs. These parents will insist that their children remain on the path because they have a place to go and a time by which they must arrive (age 18). However, they allow their children to walk anywhere on the path. Within the boundaries of the path the child is free to wander and set his own pace. Occasionally the child will need to stop and sit on the grass for a while and the GBD parent will allow them to, as long as it does not interfere in the travel plans too much. Occasionally there will be a dangerous stretch on the path and the GBD parent will determine that it is important for the child to step in certain places on the path to avoid danger. This parent will insist that safety be maintained while traveling, but once the dangerous area is passed, will allow their child to continue to choose their own steps. The GBD parent insists that forward travel be maintained on the path but allows for freedom in how the child feels about each step. It may be important that the child walk forward, but the child is allowed to not like it. As long as the forward walk is continued, the child is allowed to feel how they feel.

No attempt is made to control the inner person of the child—who is not controllable anyway. The GBD parent knows that their child will not always listen to them or follow their advice, and the GBD parent knows that there will be consequences for not listening. Unless there is imminent danger involved, the GBD parent does not feel threatened by allowing their child to suffer natural consequences. This is different from imposing a punishment (the response inflicted by an authoritarian parent who is disobeyed). If a child dawdles and is late for a birthday party and misses the cake, they miss the cake. If a child wants to see a movie but spends the money given to them for the movie on a toy, they do not get to see the movie. The child may not like the consequences, but the GBD parent knows that the child must understand that there are consequences to actions. Once an adult, the person who does not conform to what is expected of her at work will most likely lose her job, or at least will not be advanced. The person who cannot maintain their finances will face bankruptcy. These are natural consequences.[xxxiii]

Most importantly the GBD parent walks beside their child modeling how and where to walk and trusts that their child will learn what he needs to know. I once overheard an older woman telling a younger woman who was concerned with her child potty-training that she could complain to her if the child had not potty-trained by college—otherwise it would all get worked out. I liked this advice and have applied it to many things that I believe should be child-directed. These children grow up learning responsibility. They, more importantly, grow up taking into consideration the feelings of others. Because they are respected as children they respect others. They are the leaders that others want to follow because they know they can trust them to seek everyone's best interest. But they only become this way by parents who lead them and model for them what is involved in seeking the best interest of others.

Which style does God use? I believe that God is definitely a GBD parent. "This is the Way, walk ye in it." Life is a big field and non-believers are free to play anywhere in the field that they choose. God's children, believers, are instructed to stick to the path and continue moving forward. What is the path? Jesus said,

"I am the Way, the Truth, and the Life."[xxxiv] Moving forward on the path is becoming more Christ-like. The path has definite boundaries within which there is much freedom. Let's look at how God handles new Christians to see if we can find a model to follow. Maybe you remember when you were a new Christian or when you last talked to one. Didn't it seem like the world was fantastic for them and nothing could go wrong? Maybe they were even struggling with sin issues, but they were still floating. I believe this is because God is only holding them accountable to the broadest of boundaries. Essentially these boundaries are the Greatest Commandment given in Matthew 22:36-40 when Jesus said we are to love God with all our hearts, minds, souls, and strength, and love our neighbors as ourselves. What new Christian doesn't love God, themselves and others? Even Paul, in I Corinthians 3:2 explains that he has fed the Christians at Corinth with milk and not meat because they could not bear it yet.

But babies grow up. It is as we mature in Christ that more is expected of us. God brings up one issue at a time asking us to deal with it—either a relationship we need to resolve, or a sin from which we need to repent, or an attitude which needs to be corrected, etc. When we move towards being adults in Christ, we are able to handle the meat, not just the milk. God even brings out specifics in our life that are not discussed in the Bible but which are specific for our lives and our ministries. The Bible does not say whether to own a home or rent an apartment but some Christians, knowing they are called to worldwide missions, are told by God to rent so they can go at any moment. In order for a Christian to know God is telling them to rent, and to trust Him enough to do it, they need to have learned two things: 1) to recognize God's voice, and 2) to trust Him. Paul's message in Romans 14 and 15 is discussing making choices on the path of life. Essentially he says, "Work it out between you and God. If it pleases God, do it. HOWEVER, if it offends your brother, don't do it because to offend your brother is not pleasing to God." Too often I have heard this passage used to justify or restrict everything from not being a vegetarian, to not drinking alcohol, to "I can do anything I want to do." None of these is an appropriate interpretation or application of Paul's message. Paul is discussing appropriate boundaries (what pleases God and others) and having freedom within these boundaries. To wander off the path will result in consequences for the believer (premarital sex can result in pregnancy, transmission of diseases, and spiritual bondage to a person who is not your spouse). But on the path there are many places to step that are safe.

Paul discusses the development of believers as compared to the development of an infant maturing to adulthood (1 Peter 2.1-3). When a person becomes a new believer he is a baby in Christ. They are allowed to walk anywhere on the path and be safe. They are the ones who are giddy at recently having found God and He is gentle in teaching them the perimeters of the path. Often, even when they wander off the path, God blocks the consequences and quickly restores them to the path. This is where believers identify the unsafe practices of their life before Christ and deal with getting on the path. As the believer matures there will be times where they must follow a certain portion of the path to be safe. At those times, the Holy Spirit walks beside them to help them maneuver that portion of the path. Sometimes the believer will stop to rest in the grass. There may be consequences for this if they stay too long, but God will allow them to make the choice. There is freedom on the path. God is also a good God and will encourage the believer to not stay sitting too long because there is a place they are going and they need to get there. It is as the believer matures that God teaches them a more structured walk. But let's go back to our developing child to get to this point.

With infants the important thing is, as mentioned above, meeting their physical, emotional, mental, and spiritual needs while keeping them safe. If we want to parent like God, we need to help our children recognize our voice and learn to trust us. The best way to do this is by meeting their needs in the first year of life. Infants do not distinguish between needs and wants. We might understand that being held is a want for which we sometimes have to delay satisfaction, but a baby does not think that deeply. All they know is that they need to be held. I'm sure every child would love to be able to tell mom exactly what they want, but remember that crying is the only way God has given babies to communicate. A six-month old is not trying to manipulate his parents to get them to feed him. When a child cries and the parent responds, then the child learns to trust the parent. They learn that their needs will be met and that mom and dad are looking out for them. And they don't just learn to trust the parents, they learn to trust in all relationships they will have in the future. The primary relationship with the mother sets the stage for all future relationships.[xxxv] When the mother doesn't respond to the child's cries, the child learns to distrust not only the mother, but also the world. He needs to be fed and will do whatever it takes to get fed. The less he has to do, the safer he will feel. The most important lesson for an infant to learn is that life is safe. The child who learns to trust her parents becomes a calm child. She learns that she can rely on her parents and if she lets her needs be known they will be met. According to Dr. William Sears, babies who are quick to get their needs met learn to cry better, while children who are left to cry without getting their needs met learn to either cry louder, or stop crying because there is no point.[xxxvi]

Children need to learn interdependence, not independence. Interdependence is what allows a child to be fully an individual with their own healthy boundaries, and fully able to interact with others to help get their needs met and to work for the common good. A marriage of two dependent people will be dysfunctional and enmeshed. A marriage of two independent people is likely to grow apart. A marriage of two interdependent people will develop as they grow in their own interests and in the common goal of the marriage. We are responsible for preparing our children for a healthy marriage.

Developmentally, children are not ready to understand cause and effect until after the first year of life. When they begin to learn this lesson, they will learn first that some things make mommy happy, and some make her sad or mad. The child who has been nurtured and made to feel safe with her parents will want to do the things that make mommy happy. The child not nurtured by having all of her needs met will not care. The first year of life is the foundation for the rest of the child's development. The foundation can either be made of stone, a sure foundation, or sand, which will wash away at the first rain. It is this foundation from which lessons of right and wrong will spring as the child begins to learn (between the ages of 3 to 5) that the things that make mommy happy are good for them and the things that make mommy sad or mad are wrong.

When setting rules for our children, let us also follow our heavenly Father's example—instead of rules, set boundaries. Rules assume that we can control the other person. We cannot control anyone but ourselves. When we are trying to control another—including our children—we are not controlling ourselves, and we are guaranteed to be unable to control our children. They might outwardly obey, but a parent will never be able to control their child's inside—the mind, will, and emotions (the heart). God knows this because He gave us free will. But there is good news.

When we teach our children that they can trust us, they desire to please us by doing what makes us happy. As the child grows to the age-range of three to five they will begin to understand that what makes mommy and daddy happy is "good" and what makes mommy and daddy unhappy is "bad." This is the necessary step before the child can understand the concepts of "good" and "evil," an understanding that is necessary in order to understand sin. If we teach them that we are untrustworthy they will not desire to do what makes us happy because they will not care what we want. In other words—they will learn what we teach them.

Let's look at how we can model our boundary setting after God's boundary setting for us. I am suggesting a different approach than what is commonly taught. Often it is suggested that strict limits must be enforced when a child is young and then, as the child gets older, you let out the limits and grant them more freedom until you release them as adults into the world. I believe that, by following God's example, we should start with very broad boundaries for our children. As they grow, bring the boundaries in tighter with each individual child so that when they become adults and go into the world they can take with them an individual set of boundaries that can serve them in life. We don't release them into the world; we prepare them for it.

What boundaries are important for babies? I begin with safety. In our homes we are safe in every situation and at all times. I don't leave my child unattended because it isn't safe. We don't pet strange animals without the owner's permission because it isn't safe. Choices are not always made based on what is convenient or what any of us wants—they are often made over the issue of safety. If it is unsafe, we don't do it. If it is safe, then we decide based on what is convenient and what is wanted by all.

As I mentioned in our family goals, we strive to have God at the center of our lives and everything we do, then we are family-focused and are seeking the goals of every member of our family. We also try to remember that as parents and Christians we are called to sacrifice and be servants—not just to strangers, but also to our children. The greater are called serve the least and not the other way around. By putting our child's needs, and some of his wants, ahead of ours, we are teaching him to sacrifice for others. I already see the return on this investment as my son is very considerate of others and has a love for people that is genuine.

Once you start with safety you must add boundaries as the child gets older, but what boundaries do you add? There is no way to tell you what boundaries your child may need—and no boundaries will work for all children. But let's take one example and see how a boundary can change over time to reflect the changing needs and maturity level of the child. Let's look at the example of sharing as it is a fairly common parenting goal to teach this social skill to our children. Children need to learn to share, but they also must learn about property rights. It is very upsetting to a child to have her very special toy played with and more upsetting if something goes wrong. If you have a rule that the child must share it becomes very difficult to take special toys or special circumstances into consideration. When you set rules you then have to determine exceptions and it becomes burdensome to the parent. Instead, let's see how this might be done using boundaries. When the child is between two and four and is having a friend over to play I might tell him to pick five toys that will be shared with their friend. Those five toys would be taken into a room where I would be able to supervise their play and where the other toys are unavailable. It is my responsibility to protect my child; children feel safe when they can trust their parents to look out for them. This is important to remember because should my child decide that he doesn't want to share one of the five toys he selected I would take that toy and put it away. I would then explain that we are sharing five toys so he needs to pick out one to replace the one we are putting away. My child feels protected, but the boundary of sharing five toys is intact, and the children have plenty of toys for playing.

As my child gets older, for example between four and seven (again, this is individual), I would gradually move the boundary so that there are five special toys being put away and not played with and everything else can be used for play. The toys that are put away might change depending on which friend is coming over to play or what toy is preferred that day and that is fine.

The point is respecting the property rights of your child while still teaching them to share and be social.

Healthy boundaries set the stage for our lives. And, when given rules instead, children believe that the rules they were taught are the way things should always be. How difficult the first year of marriage is as two people must learn that there are different ways to do things! In our marriage, we tried to work together to come up with even better ways than either of us had been taught to do things. We could not have done this if either of us thought our way was the only right way. It is our responsibility, as parents, to teach our children appropriate behavior. At the same time, it is important to remember that what we consider "appropriate behavior" is our preference. Every parent has a different set of ideas for what is or is not appropriate behavior. In some homes it is inappropriate to jump on the bed. In other homes it is fine. Because of this, it will help your children greatly if you can teach them your preferences without teaching that this is the only way to do something. Teaching your children that different people do things differently will also help them to learn the rules in new situations, without assuming they are the same as at your house. One very easy way to accomplish this is to explain expectations by saying, "At our house...." This way you can teach your child new expectations by saying, "In this house.... " Of course there are some things that are always a matter of safety. It would not be appropriate to teach your child, "In our house we don't touch hot stoves." Your child needs to understand that it is not safe to ever touch hot stoves. So say that. "It is never safe to touch hot stoves." Who wants a child to need to touch every hot stove to determine if it too is not safe? Rather than, "At our house we don't run into the street without looking," a child needs to understand, "It is not safe to run into the street without looking." This will be the same wherever your child is playing.

Now, within healthy boundaries there will still be times when, as the parent, the authority, you will need to insist that things are done. It is possible to do so without violating your child's will, emotions, or personhood. I would like to get to what I consider the most practical part of this book. I am going to give you Five Steps to help your child to do what needs to be done as well as several other tools for practicing Grace-Based Discipline. This is a very important lesson because, while I believe it is important to respect our children and not to control them, you are the parents and you will ultimately be deciding what needs to be done.

The Five Steps

These Five Steps are one of the most effective things I learned while working in the Early Childhood Ministry at Word of Grace in Mesa, Arizona, mentoring under Lisa Kuzara Seibold, the Minister of Early Childhood Education. It was amazing to me that by using these steps I was able to work with any child, no matter how compliant or how difficult, and earn their respect and obedience within one to three days. When my husband worked in the classroom with me he was hesitant to use the steps because he thought they sounded weird and he couldn't believe they would work. When he finally did, he was amazed at how effective they are. So, without further ado …

"You need to stop yourself from doing _____." OR "You need to _____." And then give a reason.

Example: "You need to stop yourself from walking with scissors. That is not safe." OR "You need to sit down with the scissors. You are not being safe."

Then, if they don't stop, or start doing it again:

Get their attention, look them in the eye, and, if necessary, get down on their level and say, "Listen to my words, 'You need _____.'"

And tell them what to do instead.

Example: "Listen to my words, 'You need to stop yourself from walking with the scissors. Either set them down, or sit down yourself and use them at the table.'"

Then, if it continues:

"You are having a hard time stopping yourself. Can you stop yourself, or do you need my help?"

And let your child answer. If they say they need your help, help them. Remove the scissors from their hand and/or help them sit down at the table where it is safe to have the scissors.

If they say they can stop themselves, let them try. If they can't:

"You're having a very hard time stopping yourself. Here, let me help you."

Then you move in and help the child as stated in Step Number Three.

The Bear Hug

This step is the highest step and is to be used when your child resists your help or at any time during the steps if your child becomes out-of-control. By this I mean she is unable to control herself and might hurt someone. Stand behind your child and put your arms over her shoulders and crossed over her chest. Your hands can be used, if necessary, to hold her arms so that no one gets hit. Slight pressure can be put on the child's shoulders to hold their feet down on the ground so that she cannot kick or try to run away. You are standing behind your child so while holding her this way you can speak softly into her ear—rather than yelling in her face while looking down on her. When this happens, the child usually relaxes into your body and you can feel the tension leave her body. At the least, she will be more willing to listen to your instructions.

As you get to know your child you can cut out unnecessary steps and go to the step you know your child needs. This may mean going from Step One to Step Four—where you move in to help them. As your child grows, you may only have to use Step One. You may add steps back in that were skipped when your child was younger. Older children find great satisfaction in not needing help. It is very important to always use at least step one and to use this tool to the fullest. You don't want to reduce this tool to a means of demanding empty rules compliance. You want to use it to shape your child's self-discipline and you need to approach your child with the belief that they desire self-discipline and want to cooperate. Help is not a punishment. Help is simply help.

There is a great deal going on when you tell a child "You need to stop yourself." You are making the decision about what will be done, but you are putting responsibility for doing it on your child. This is important because you will not always be present to make your child behave. What we need to teach our children is self-control. The only way they will be controlling themselves is when they can stop themselves. It is also amazing how young a child can be and still respond to these phrases. My children begin hearing these words at birth so they know them when they are able to respond. This way I don't have to guess when they're ready to hear them. When they do understand them they stop themselves. They start out learning that this is expected of them.

Let's look at an example. You need to leave for an appointment and your child is playing with a toy. Give her a five-minute warning so that she can finish her play. This is not a method you can use if you are going to wait until the last minute and expect your child to jump-to. You must begin getting your child ready at least twenty minutes early, which means you must be ready early also. How would this look?

"Emily, you have five minutes to finish your play and then it is time to go in the car."

Wait five minutes. If your child needs reminder warnings then do three- and one-minute warnings.

"Emily, you need to stop yourself from playing and clean up your toy. It is time to go."

Wait a minute and if she does, great. You get to go early. If she doesn't, get down on her level, look in her eyes and say,

"Listen to my words, you need to stop yourself from playing. It's time to clean up your toy. We need to leave."

Then give her a chance to do it. Your child may need you to touch their shoulder and get their attention first. Give them this courtesy. If she doesn't stop herself, say to her,

"You're having a hard time stopping yourself. Can you stop yourself or do you need my help?"

Wait for her to answer or to show that she won't be stopping herself. If she needs your help, help her. This does not mean punish her. It means, move in and help her put the toys away. Respect that she is having a hard time leaving her fun play and help her physically make the transition. If she says she can stop herself, give her a chance to do it. However, if she doesn't, move in anyway.

"Here, let me help you."

And do. Now, if she begins throwing a fit, which normal, healthy children are apt to do when you won't let them have their way, there is no reason to get angry with her. She is not doing it to you. She is doing it in reaction to what you are doing to her. And remember, you can stop behavior but you have no control over what is going on inside.

So, move in with the Bear Hug. Remember to get down on her level so that you are behind her speaking softly in her ear. Let her know that this is unacceptable behavior and that you will let her go as soon as she has stopped herself. Remind her that you are doing this because she is not stopping herself and she needs your help. And reflect her feelings.

Reflecting Feelings

This seems like a good place to discuss the idea of reflecting feelings. Dr. Gaim Ginott, in his book <u>Between Parent & Child</u>, introduces the idea of reflecting feelings. Oftentimes children are satisfied when they know that you understand how they feel. That alone is enough to change their behavior. Sometimes, children don't know how they feel. They don't have the adult language that would allow them to cognitively say to you, "Mom, I'm feeling rather angry that you took away my toy. I'm also depressed because you did not replace it with something fun for me to do. By the way, that pizza at lunch made me feel rather off-balance because I think I might be allergic to dairy." (I know, that's a whole different book, but keep the potential of allergies in mind when a behavior change occurs within thirty minutes of eating a food.) So, instead of saying these things, they act out. They might start a fight with a sibling or be mean to the dog. They might sit in their room and do nothing for a long period of time. As their parent, they are looking to you to help them understand what they are feeling and what to do about it. This is when you reflect their feelings.

When you stop your child's play and he begins to sulk you might say to him, "I see that you are disappointed that I stopped your play." Then see what he says. He might agree and restate this idea in his own words, or he might say that he is not disappointed but will begin a dialogue with you that will uncover his true feelings. Reflecting feelings is simply putting your child's obvious feelings into words. Many times children do not have the language of feelings to use to describe how they feel. It is our responsibility as parents to teach this language to them (and learn it ourselves if no one has taught us). Children need to learn how to say, "I am angry," just as much as they need to learn how to say, "I am happy." Even though we would prefer to hear the latter, both are important for communication and understanding to exist between two individuals—parent and child or spouse to spouse.

This language of feelings is especially important if a child is ever going to work through conflict with another child. Some would argue that children should never be allowed to quarrel and others would say that if left alone children work everything out themselves. I would propose a middle-of-the-road approach on this one.

Conflict Resolution

I do not believe that "fighting" is appropriate between any two individuals—children or adults. But there will always be differences of opinions. This is normal and healthy. We are all different people and we have a right to different views. However, with all rights come responsibilities and we have a responsibility to express our different views in a healthy way. As parents, it is our responsibility to teach our children how to communicate differing views in a healthy way. This happens first through modeling, when we have differing views from other adults in our children's presence, second through expressing ourselves in a healthy way when we disagree with our children, and third by helping them work through conflict between themselves and other children. How? How do we mediate between children while helping them share their feelings and work out disagreements, including helping them work out solutions, without telling them what to do? The answer comes with a combination of reflecting feelings, providing words, and questions, questions, questions. Let me give you an example so you can see this idea in action.

Tommy has hit Billy who is crying and trying to hit Tommy back. You see what has happened so there is no question about who did what. You first step is to stop Billy from being able to hit Tommy. It isn't "fair" that Tommy got to hit Billy and Billy doesn't get to hit Tommy, but a parent's job is not to make things "fair." If Billy points out this lack of fairness, you tell him that sometimes things are not fair and it is your job to make sure that everyone is safe. You may add that you will also not allow Tommy to hit Billy again. Depending upon how upset Billy is you may need to put him in the Bear Hug until he is calm enough to participate in communication with Tommy.

Once he has calmed down enough, kneel down to the level of the two children with one arm around each of them. Move them, if necessary, so that they are looking at each other. It is important, in this instance, to NOT ask what happened. You saw what happened and you do not want to make the conversation prolonged or confused by giving them the opportunity to try and make themselves look better or worse off by giving their version of what happened. Instead, tell them what you saw happen. "Tommy, I saw you hit Billy." Then turn to Billy and ask him, "Billy, how did you feel when Tommy hit you?" Billy may be able to tell you, and he may not. If he is unable to tell you, help by providing him words. "Are you angry? Are your feelings hurt?" Give him a couple of options for responses and then let him choose which best expresses his feelings. Once he has, have him look at Tommy, while Tommy looks at him, and tell him, "You need to tell Tommy how you felt when he hit you. And, Tommy, look at Billy while he tells you."

Now you need to ask Tommy, "Did you hear what Billy said? You hurt his feelings when you hit him. You also hurt his arm. Did you mean to do that?" You may be surprised to find that usually children did not intend the result of their actions. When they hit they may have wanted the toy the other child was playing with, but, obviously, they hurt the feelings, and perhaps the body, of the other child. Do not assume that the child is lying if they say they didn't mean to hurt their friend. To an adult there may be an obvious connection between hitting and hurting, but to a child there isn't. Once he has admitted that he didn't mean to hurt his friend, it is time to ask him if he would like to apologize. Do not make him apologize. If a child is forced to apologize when they are not sorry, they are being taught to lie. However, if the child admits that they do want to apologize, give him the words to do it. "Then tell Billy that you are sorry." After the apology, give Billy the opportunity to accept Tommy's apology and forgive him. Forgiving someone who has wronged us is as much a life lesson, especially in a Christian home, as is learning how to ask for forgiveness. This can be accomplished by simply asking Billy, "Do you accept Tommy's apology?" If he says "yes," then they are off to playing again. If he says "no," then maybe they need to be separated in their play until they are ready to come together again. Do not treat this as a punishment.

You cannot force someone to forgive another, but if they are friends, they will eventually not want to play apart any longer.

At the same time, if you had asked Tommy if he meant to hurt Billy and he said that he did, this is a time for you, as the adult, to intervene in the communication. You can simply inform Tommy, "I am telling you that it is not acceptable for you to hit." Then ask him if he can play with Billy without hitting. If he says he can, let him and be ready to intervene if he cannot stop himself.

In the example above you saw what happened. If you didn't see what happened you may choose to ask what happened, but once you get an idea you can stop the story telling. If you don't they may start trying to convince you of how justified they are in their actions. This may especially be true if one child hit the other for having said something hurtful. One rule we do have is, "We don't hurt with our bodies or our words." I would repeat this rule and then move them into the discussion for resolving the hurt feelings.

If this is a recurring problem between the two boys, make sure that you are closely supervising their play and be ready to intervene, if at all possible, before there is an opportunity for violence. If your child, or the other child, has a propensity for violent behavior (or not sharing, or grabbing another child's toys, or any other unacceptable playtime behavior) it is an unrealistic expectation to expect that the child will not do it this time. Always hope for the best. Children will grow up and change, but always be prepared to intervene if necessary.

Descriptive Praise

Before I share any other tools I want to discuss Descriptive Praise. Many people praise their children by saying things like "Nice picture," "Good job," and "How beautiful." This praise is meaningless at its best and manipulative at its worst. Words like "nice," "good," and "beautiful" are very subjective and praise like this encourages children to try to please others instead of doing things for their intrinsic value. It puts the value and worth of them, their actions, and their creations in the judgment of another. Instead try using Descriptive Praise. In simple terms, this is describing what you see to a child so that they see the value is inherent in them, their actions and their creations. If your child brings you a picture tell them what you see. "You used lots of green. I see squiggly lines and some straight ones." If your daughter asks what you think of her dress tell her what you see. "It's blue and it has flowers." You will be amazed at how her face lights up. My son calls me into his playroom to show me what he's done with his cars and I tell him what I see. "You have lined them up and all the trucks are together." He feels a sense of accomplishment and knows that I have noticed his hard work because I can tell him what he did.

If you have a history of using non-descriptive praise then you may need to start with lots of descriptive praise until your child's sense of value and worth becomes rooted in her own value. If your child comes out and asks you if you like something because you aren't telling them you do you can turn this around too. Try saying, "I can see that you like it." Or try saying, "Do you like it?" If they say "Yes," then tell them, "That's what's important." It is also important to remember that your feelings can be conveyed by your tone of voice. Try saying, "Look at all the green," in different tones. You can express approval or disapproval depending upon your tone of voice.

A child who is used to receiving your praise may think that you don't like what they are showing you. I would go so far as to tell them, "What I think doesn't really matter. You worked hard on that picture and I'm proud of you. A picture's true value is in what you put of yourself into it. I can see a lot of you in this picture." This might even be an excellent opportunity to teach about art (or whatever they've brought for your approval) and all of the different styles that different people like. Ask them which styles they prefer and share where you agree and disagree. Explain that art is about the artists expressing themselves. There is still a place for being genuine with your child. If you are impressed, say so. It's the non-genuine, non-descriptive praise that I'm hoping you'll replace. Every artist loves to have his art speak to someone, but he creates his art for himself.

The greatest danger from non-descriptive praise is that it can block your child's movement from pleasing you to pleasing God. Children who receive praise from their parents get caught up in striving to please men. Descriptive praise puts value on character and the motivation for the actions. Through descriptive praise we teach our children to strive to please God. We point out the character qualities that God desires and put the value on the presence of these qualities.

This can be seen in the use of "good job" which many parents have used to replace "good boy/girl." While this is an improvement in that it doesn't directly attach a child's worth to their behavior, it still puts an emphasis on your opinion of their actions. Ask yourself, what about what they've done is "good?" Tell them that instead. "You were very cooperative." "You worked hard until the job was finished, even when you wanted to stop." "You sure handled that in a creative way. I would never have thought to do it that way."

There are other tools that I would like to share with you, but the only requirement for a tool is that it show your child love and respect. You are only limited by your imagination and I hope that what I share here will be a springboard for you to come up with tools that work for your child.

Dances[xxxviixxxviii]

Instead of thinking your daughter needs to control her physical energy by putting her in Time Out[xxxix] and making her sit still, respect her need to move and release energy. Dancing is a wonderful way to physically express big emotions. Do an angry dance.

Do a happy dance. Get your child up and moving and getting their energy out in a healthy way. Do this anywhere—home or car. Imagine turning your daughter's tantrum at leaving a playgroup into a family angry dance as you bop down the road. Turn up the radio or make up a song to fit the emotion. "If you're angry and you know it stomp your feet...." "I'm so happy! I'm so happy! I'm so happy! Stomp! Stomp! Stomp!"

Pictures[xl]

Art is an expression for the world of what we feel on the inside. If your son is having a big emotion suggest he express it in art. "Draw how happy you are." "What does your anger look like?" Remember to use descriptive praise when you see their picture. "Wow, your anger is very black with lots of strong lines." "Look at how happy you are. I see lots of yellow and pink and so many squiggly lines!" Creative art is the precursor to language arts and not only will you be helping your son to express his feelings in a healthy way you will be moving him along the path of writing and language skills. Don't punish for emotions; teach your child how to express them.

The Comfort Corner[xli]

Choose a corner of your main living space and let your children help you decorate it. Include a child-sized chair, pillows, quiet toys and books. When your daughter is having a difficult time dealing with her emotions or is having big emotions to a request you've made or to a change then suggest they go to the Comfort Corner. They can go alone or they can ask you to go (which is where the "cuddle" part comes in). She can lie down and rest; read a book; play with toys; think things through for herself; cuddle you if she so desires; just take a break. When she is refreshed she can come back and deal with things much better. Time Out typically isolates a child from other people and can be shaming and tormenting for the extroverted child. While in the Comfort Corner, she still has access to other people. There is no isolation. There is no shame. Isolation and shame do not teach life skills. However, learning to remove yourself from a stressful situation until you can return and deal with it in a healthy way is a very valuable skill.

Say to your daughter, "You are having a hard time listening to my words right now. You need to go to the Comfort Corner and take a break. Would you like me to come with you?" Validating. Sensitive. Loving and respectful. A child having a hard time listening to and respecting an adult's requests is not feeling safe and secure and needs the opportunity to regroup. Give her that; don't punish her for having those feelings.

The Problem Place[xlii]

This tool is wonderful for use after you have helped children learn how to resolve conflict in the ways that I suggested earlier. Once they have the tools to solve problems, let them. Determine a place that is set apart from activity and when children are fighting over something—a toy, an activity, what show to watch on T.V., anything—have them go to the Problem Place until they come up with a solution. Try to resist helping them find a solution. The rules for the Problem Place are no hurting and respect one another. As long as they are respecting the rules let them work things out themselves. When children discover their own solutions to a problem they are more likely to abide by the solution. When a parent imposes their own solution on a situation they are more likely to be met with resistance. One thing that is difficult, but very important, is to respect your children's solution, no matter how silly it seems to you. If it was an effective solution and it works then that is what matters. This helps them develop problem-solving skills. If a solution doesn't work they will be unlikely to try to repeat it in the future. If need be, send them back to the Problem Place to come up with a new solution.

Five-Minute Warnings

When you are expecting to have your son make a transition give him the respect of letting him know ahead of time. Give him a five-minute warning that tells him there are five minutes left before it is time to go or change activities. "Five minutes until we have to go. Get your ideas out." Maybe let him know that he has time to do one more idea. Time to go down the slide five more times. Time to color one more picture. Time is very intangible for children and this is a practical way to help them understand how long until they are expected to change gears and do a different activity. If you are true to allowing five minutes for a warning then you will be helping them develop their concept of time and transitions will be made easier. Your son may need more warnings. Be willing to offer three- and one-minute warnings if things will go more smoothly.

1, 2, 3 Transition

Children, especially toddlers, often have a difficult time making transitions. Toddlers struggle with stopping play to have a diaper change. Children of all ages don't want to leave a playdate when they are having fun. It is important to give warnings. 1, 2, 3 Transition is useful at the time a change is being made. Tell your daughter that you will count to three and that is how long she has to make the necessary transition. For example, if you want to change your daughter's diaper and this is normally a difficult time for her, then tell her, "It is time to change your diaper. Please decide where you want me to change it. I will count to three and then you need to lie down. If you don't lay down then I will help you and I get to decide where we change the diaper." Even the most independent and headstrong toddler will be motivated to keep the control given to them in this situation by choosing a place and laying down for the diaper change. If she is tired or emotions are already high then you may need to help her, but reminding your daughter why you are helping her to find a place to lie down will encourage her to accept your help. At first she may wait until you've counted to three before she lies down. Let her. Just remind her that you've reached three and that she needs to lie down. Guiding her independence in this way can be difficult, but will pay off with great rewards when you want to enlist her help in more difficult things.

"It's time to go now. I'm going to count to three. You need to be heading for the door by the time I reach three or I will help you to the door." "It's time to turn off the T.V. You have to the count of three to turn it off otherwise I will turn it off." And remember that "helping" isn't a punishment. In fact, if you go to turn off the T.V. and she decides to do it, let her. Remind her that she needs to do it when you ask next time, but let her decide this time to cooperate. Respect and appreciate any choice to cooperate. And if you help her by turning it off, don't make it a punishment by lecturing or yelling at her for not doing it herself. She was given a choice and chose. Respect her choice.

This is not a punishment and it is not a countdown to a punishment. It's a tangible timeframe in which your daughter is given the opportunity to do something herself. "Helping" is never a punishment and she should never fear help from you. Helping her is an acknowledgement that you have asked too much from her at this time and you are willing to do what you must to help her fulfill your request.

This is not an all-inclusive list of tools. You are limited only by your imagination. Use the Grace-Based Discipline Window, which I will introduce in the next chapter to develop more tools for your toolbox. The important part of any tool is that it shows love and respect. God is about relationship. I have seen the Five Steps work with children of varying ages and temperaments and be highly successful with all of them. Expect using these steps to produce improvement in your child's behavior in direct proportion to how crazy you have allowed things to already become. The other tools will also be helpful in different situations. If your child believes there are no safe boundaries and anything goes, or nothing goes, then you will have more effort to put into changing your relationship. But be persistent. This method of parenting requires a lot more of the parent than simply attempting to control your child through spanking and other punishments. Nothing worthwhile is ever easy and this effort will produce rewards that make it all worthwhile. Of course, the decision is yours, not mine, but I strongly recommend the effort. With consistency, and hard work, you will see the rewards.

The Tools in Public

Once I have determined what is important in my home for my children, I am faced with the experiences of my children in other people's homes, and their children in mine. If I understand my "house rules" to be the way I prefer things to be I will be open to working with other parents in different situations. How? And where does my authority end, and theirs begin? I want to introduce what I call "Active Parenting."

Let me begin by suggesting a healthy boundary for determining responsibility and authority:

1) The parent is responsible for their child.

2) The "other" is responsible for their person and property.

This distinction does away with what is often a very fuzzy line for both adults and children over who is "in charge." Who has not witnessed two adults and one child together and when the "other" asks the child to do something the child turns to the parent and asks (or looks as if to ask), "Do I have to?" It may appear that the child is challenging the authority of the "other," but the child is actually asking a very good question, "Who is in authority over me in this situation?" If, as a parent, you are not sure, how will you respond to your child?

Because the "other" is responsible for their own person and property, they have the right to set rules about behavior in relation to each. In other words, they have the right to set their own "house rules." This is appropriate. If the "other" is also a parent, they have the right to enforce those "house rules" with their own children because as a parent they are responsible for their child. Now, while they are responsible for their home, they are not responsible for your child. The only way another adult can be responsible for your child is if you place your child under their authority. I recommend doing this as rarely as possible and only when the "other" is the teacher of your child's class, a babysitter/day care provider or the parent of another child with whom your child plays without you in their home. At all other times, you, as a parent, are present.

When you are present, you are responsible for your child. The less your child is without you the less this will be a concern for you.

You have a choice to make when you and your child are presented with the "other's" "house rules." As a parent who is "Active Parenting," you will either both *affirm* the rule and *enforce* it with your child, or you will *diffuse* it. To *affirm* it means that you agree with the rule and see its value in being enforced. To *enforce* it means that you verbally and/or physically agree with the "other" that this is a rule to be followed. For example, the "other" gives your child food and states that children, in their home, are to eat at the table or on the floor. You, as the parent, then actively state, "Okay, let's go sit at the table (or on the floor)," and then, depending on the child's age, help the child get situated or even pick up your child and move them. By doing this you have maintained your authority over your child in the situation while respecting the rules of the "other" for eating in their home.

In order to understand the concept of *diffuse*, let me explain two different types of diffusers. The first type is an essential oil diffuser. This works by placing a concentrated essential oil with water in the diffuser. When turned on, the diffuser mists the water and the oil mixture into the air. Before being put into the diffuser the oil is concentrated; after the diffuser it is such a light mist that one does not feel it on their person. The other diffuser is for hair dryers. The air coming out of a hair dryer moves hard and fast in one direction. The diffuser is put on the hair dryer and, because it has lots of holes, it changes the direction and the strength of the air. When you act as a diffuser for the "other's" rules, you will be doing one of these two things. Like the hair dryer diffuser, you may be changing and softening the application of the rule to your child. Like the essential oil diffuser, you may be diluting the effects of rule so that they do not affect your child.

Let's look at how this distinction works when applied to real situations. If you are eating dinner at a friend's home and the "other" states a rule in their home for children to eat all of their vegetables. You must first respect their right to make and enforce this rule as it applies to their own children. But if you do not make your child eat foods they don't like, you may choose to *diffuse* this rule in one of two ways. You might say, "Susan, you don't like green beans so you don't have to eat them, but you can eat all of your carrots." This is acting as the hair dryer diffuser. You softened the rule by not making your child eat a vegetable they don't like, and you changed the direction by agreeing that Susan can eat all of her carrots. You might also say, especially if a vegetable your child does not like is the only option, "In our family we don't have to eat foods we don't like." This makes a distinction between family preferences, does not lessen the effect of the rule on their own children, but takes away the rules' effects on your child. This is what I call the essential oil diffuser. It is important to remember that you are not challenging the "other's" rule; you are only lessening its effects on your child. Their right to make the rule remains intact. Their right to enforce this rule for their own children remains intact.

I would like to look at an example and how each of the above approaches might look. You take your child to your friend's house for the afternoon and she puts on a video in the family room for the children to watch while you will be talking in the dining room. The children are then instructed to stay in the family room without bothering you until the video is over. You have a choice to make. You may:

1) Decide to *affirm* your friend's decision and enforce it for your child by saying something like, "That's right Andrew, you need to stay in the family room until the video is over," and then follow your friend to the dining room. OR

2) Decide to *diffuse* the rule by saying, "Andrew, stay in here and watch the video, but if you need me, you come and get me." (The hair dryer diffuser) OR

3) You don't like the chosen video, don't want your child watching T.V., don't like how the children get along without an adult present, or for whatever reason. You may decide to *diffuse* the situation by saying, "Andrew, you need to come with me into the dining room and play with a toy in there." (The essential oil diffuser)

Yes, you are in your friend's home, but you are Andrew's parent. You do not have to allow him to do something you do not want him to do, just because your friend has set a rule for her children.

It is also important to remember that you are sure of two things if you are leaving your child in someone else's authority. The first is that you trust the "other" with the care of your child. I have seen parents leave their children with people they don't know, other children (teenagers), the closest day care or the one with availability, without any question of whether this "other" is teaching in agreement with them and respecting their child in the same way they do. Too often children are being obedient to childcare providers who are not being safe or are harming the child. The second is that you prepare your child for being under someone else's authority. This should be done verbally by explaining to your child that you, as the parent, trust this "other" and you expect your child to listen to them and cooperate with them. By making a clear distinction between when you are actively parenting, and when you are turning over your authority, you will help your child answer the question, "Who is 'in charge' of me right now?"

This is a very important question for children to have answered for reasons beyond knowing what behavior is acceptable. The answer to this question will determine how safe your child feels in public. If they believe they are at the whim of every adult they will not feel as safe as if they believe you will protect them from the unreasonable requests of other adults. This allows your child to go about their business of playing, exploring, and learning without worrying about having to please every adult with whom they come into contact. They can trust that you are looking out for their best interest.

Chapter Six
The Window

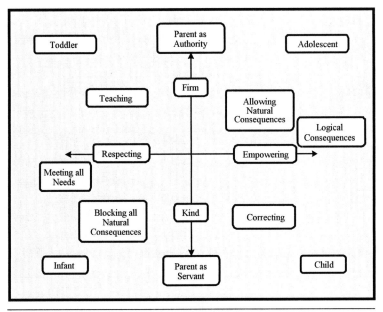

Figure 1: The Window

You can take any discipline idea to this window and see if it fits within the parameters of Grace-Based Discipline.

Let's look first at the various parenting styles. On a continuum of permissive to punitive (or authoritarian-style parenting) let's imagine permissive parenting on

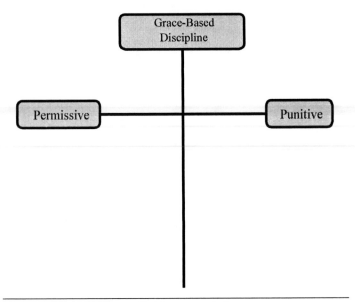

Figure 2: Our cross to bear.

the far left and punitive on the far right. Grace-Based Discipline falls directly in the center of the continuum and we will mark it with a straight line. This symbolizes the cross that is to be at the center of a believer's life. It is around this cross that we construct our window. (See Figure 2)

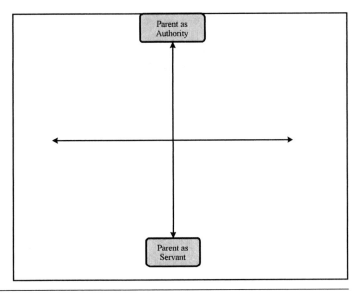

Figure 3: Parental Role

Because our cross to bear is to strive to be Christ-like, even in our parenting, we will add to the picture the qualities of "Parent as Authority" and "Parent as Servant." Christ is our authority who acted as our servant. We are in authority over our children but are called to serve them in following Christ's example. See **Figure 3** for a depiction of how parental authority fits into the window.

As a parent you will need to act both as authority and servant, but choosing which way is to take priority will depend upon the age of your child and what you are trying to accomplish. Your role in any given situation is part of the equation for determining which tool will be the most effective for you and for your child. It will also determine whether your primary response needs to be "kind" or "firm."

A servant is kind. An authority is firm. As a parent you must be both, but sometimes you need to emphasize kindness and other times you need to be firmer. One of the most difficult aspects of parenting is determining which role you should be in.

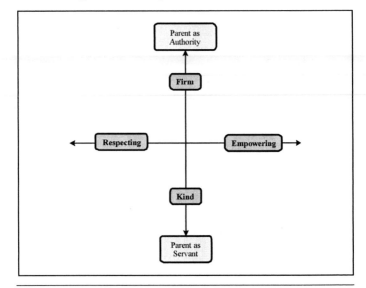

Figure 4: Parental Qualities.

The next part of the equation is the age of the child. We will consider the four stages of "Infant," "Toddler," "Child" and "Adolescent." There are no clear-cut ages for each of these stages so they operate more as a continuum of their own. One thing to remember is that if a child's behavior seems inappropriate and immature they are likely feeling younger that day and should be approached from the younger area of the window. For example, if a three year old is being responsible and mature then it is a "Toddler" day and the "Parent as Authority" would be the appropriate role for you. If, however, your three year old is behaving in a way that feels clingy, whiny or needy then her needs that day are "Infant" needs and you will want to approach her from your role of "Parent as Servant." To try and act as the authority on days like this will only wound your child's spirit and will frustrate you. Operating from the role of "Parent as Servant" during a toddler's independent days will also create frustration. An independent little girl yelling, "Me do it!" doesn't want Mommy doing it for her. This also is in operation between the child and adolescent stages. A child will need more help than an adolescent. These four stages are in the four smaller rectangles closest to the center of the cross. But what will you be choosing to do? Each stage of development in your child will require a different emphasis in your parenting. This will be another continuum because, as we've already discussed, the stages are on a continuum. As a parent you will need to accomplish making the transition from "Blocking all Natural Consequences" for your infant to "Allowing all Natural Consequences" for your adolescent. You will do this by "Teaching" (the emphasis in the "Toddler" stage) and "Correcting" (the emphasis in the "Child" stage). You emphasize

"Teaching" with a toddler so that he is learning your expectations and how to do things. This will prepare him for the "Correcting" which will occur as a child. When your son is a "Toddler" and wants to help you everyone will be best served by taking a few minutes to show him how to do something correctly. When he is older and doing things on his own you will need to "Correct" his errors. If he has never learned what to do you will have nothing to correct. Too many parents don't take the time to teach their toddlers and are surprised when their children don't know how to do anything. This creates a childhood of punishing rather than correcting. What should be emphasized in each section is in a green box to remind you to give the green light to these parenting choices.

Can you go too far? Yes. In each phase you want to make sure you stay within the window. I want to add two more boxes to our window to show the actions that would be at the permissive and punitive edges of Grace-Based Discipline and where they fit in our window. In fact an action can be permissive or Grace-Based and an action can be punitive or Grace-Based depending on whether it is approached from within the window or from without. The two examples I give are "Meeting All Needs" and "Logical Consequences."

When your son is an infant it is appropriate, necessary even, that you meet all of his needs. For an infant, his wants are his needs. Meeting all of your infant son's needs is well within the Grace-Based Discipline Window. However, meeting all of your older child's needs is very permissive. To do everything for your older child is to keep them from taking responsibility for themselves. Each child will be ready for different things at different times so on the journey from infant to adolescent you will continue meeting some needs but stop meeting others. When your son is seven and comes in asking for food, you may need to suggest what he can make, but he will be capable of making his own sandwich (assuming you have taught him how). If you are meeting all of the needs of your adolescent then you are not allowing him to grow up and accept responsibility. But how far towards the punitive end of the spectrum do you want to go?

When your child enters adolescence she should be ready to handle more and more of the natural consequences for her choices. As an adult she will have the privilege and responsibility of experiencing them all. A healthy adult does not look for others to always bail her out. This is where logical consequences might also be an appropriate parenting tool. As your daughter prepares for her sixteenth birthday she may be ready to get her driver's license. You may decide that she must pay for her own insurance and you might talk about where she will work to earn the money. A healthy boundary for a parent to set with regards to their vehicle is that no one without insurance may drive their car. Tell your daughter in advance, perhaps at a family meeting, what will happen if she doesn't keep up the insurance payments. I suggest that she not be allowed to drive your car without insurance. If she misses a payment, take her license and keys. When she catches up the premiums, return them. This is not punitive. It is logic an adolescent can follow, and it prevents the natural consequence of being in an accident without insurance or a ticket for the same, and your daughter knows the consequences beforehand. This same action would be punitive if done reactively. If you've never discussed what will happen if she doesn't keep up the premiums, it's punitive to enter her room and demand her keys. Everything within the window needs to be proactive, not reactive.

At the same time, logical consequences applied to a toddler or even an infant is extremely punitive. A toddler does not have the logic of an adult so should not be expected to understand consequences that are based on that logic. If your toddler is swinging a stick around and is at risk for hurting someone or breaking something you will need to teach him not to do this by telling him he needs to stop himself from swinging the stick. If he does not stop then you will need to help him by taking the stick away. But this does not need to be presented as a logical consequence. Instead, look at the "Toddler" square on the spectrum. When parenting a "Toddler" you are to be parenting as the "Authority" and being "Firm," "Teaching" your toddler while "Respecting" him. When a toddler cannot stop himself from doing something you have told him to stop doing then you need to recognize that he is behaving more as an "Infant." Go then to the "Infant" window and see that you are to parent as a "Servant" and be "Kind" while

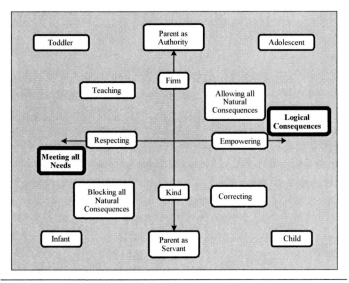

Figure 5: The Complete Window

"Respecting" and "Blocking Natural Consequences." It is in this way that you remove the stick.

Our two extremes of "Meeting All Needs" and "Logical Consequences" are thickly bordered boxes to remind you to STOP and consider whether or not you need to use an extreme approach. Make sure you are dealing with a child of the appropriate age for the extreme to be within the Window and that you are being proactive and not reactive.

This window does not contain all of the tools but you can see that taking each of the tools to the window will reveal when it would be appropriate to use. For example, let's look at The Problem Place. Sending an infant to The Problem Place would be ridiculous. For one, she couldn't get herself there and if you put her there she would not be able to do what is required to problem-solve. When she becomes a toddler and you are "Teaching" her you will want to introduce her to both the skills of problem solving and The Problem Place. If she is having a conflict with her friend go with them both to The Problem Place where you will help them work through their problem and come up with their own solution. You would do this as the "Authority" and be "Firm" that a solution is required while "Respecting" both children in finding a solution. When she becomes an older child you can simply "Correct" a situation that has become a conflict by telling both children to take it to The Problem Place. In this way you are approaching the situation as a "Servant" who offers a direction in a "Kind" way and directs both children to The Problem Place while "Empowering" them to find a solution. By the time your daughter is an adolescent you can trust that she will have the skills to solve a problem and will know when these skills are needed. While it may take some time to get used to thinking in a non-punitive way, I hope that this window will help you create ideas for this new approach to parenting.

Chapter Seven

No Greater Love—

Sacrifice in Parenting

For a long time I have referred to the style of parenting I do as "attachment parenting," also known as AP. This came from the idea in parenting that everything you are doing is designed to help a child create attachments to people and not to things, or "mother substitutes" (blankets, stuffed animals, pacifiers, etc.). Unfortunately, it has come to my attention recently that women are calling themselves attachment parents who are doing things that I do not advocate. Some of them are even counterproductive to the goal of developing an attachment with your child. There is also a large void in attachment parenting after the child reaches 16-18 months and the practicalities of what discipline should look like becomes a real question. In attachment parenting it seems that everything and anything goes covering the full range from permissive through authoritarian. For this reason,

I was challenged to come up with a more accurate name for the style of parenting that I practice and teach. The name I have come up with after much consideration is "covenant parenting."

When my husband and I were engaged I studied a great deal about covenants, specifically Jewish covenants. We actually had a Jewish/Christian Covenant Ceremony when we married. Covenants are much more serious than contracts—a term more familiar in our culture. Contracts state what each person will give up and what each person expects to receive from a relationship. Each person has to give "equal consideration" in order for a contract to be valid. That means that each person must receive as much as they give up. Otherwise, the contract is unbalanced and will not be held up in a court of law. In a covenant, however, each party agrees to give up everything for the sake of the relationship. The idea is that if both persons are giving up everything, all needs of both will be met. In reality, however, this is not always the case. Often, one person is called upon to give everything for the other and receive nothing in return. There have been many times in our marriage when either my husband or I have been called to give completely of ourselves in order to benefit the other. Because we are both giving up everything, the small things have tended to even out over time. But how do things even out for the spouse who is called upon to wait sacrificially on the dying person who will never be able to repay their effort? In a contract marriage the person called on to sacrifice might decide that they are getting nothing while giving everything and that is too much to ask. Many dying people in our culture are abandoned to hospitals or other agencies because they are too much of a bother. In a covenant relationship, this is not a valid option.

When the Israelites would enter into a covenant relationship they would kill an animal, cut it in two halves, and walk between the two halves. What they were saying was, essentially, "Be it unto me as it is to this animal if I ever break my covenant with you." When a man entered into a covenant he was putting at risk everything he owned, including his own life, to benefit the other person. When a man marries, the Bible speaks very strongly about his obligation to his wife when it says, "For this cause a man shall leave his father and his mother, and shall cleave to his wife; and they shall become one flesh."[xliii] The man is required to give up everything in order to become covenanted to his wife.

The Jewish people are covenanted to God as His people. No matter what they did or how badly they broke His heart, he is bound to them. Throughout history He has rescued them and kept them an intact nation, even without a country to provide them with boundaries for many years. This is unheard of in any other nation of people and a very interesting subject of reading and research. As Christians, we have a covenant relationship with God that is a new covenant. Jesus allowed himself to be a sacrifice, split open for our sake so that we might have a way to enter into relationship with God. "Jesus said to him, 'I am the way, and the truth, and the life; no one can come to the Father, but *through* me.'"[xliv] When we approach God through Jesus, we have entered into a covenant with God. This is why Paul can say with confidence, "If we are faithless, He remains faithful; for He cannot deny Himself."[xlv] Even if we do not hold up our end of the covenant, God is faithful and will hold up His end. This is how we can have confidence in our salvation. Without an understanding of how seriously God takes His commitment to us, we will never have confidence in our eternal relationship with Him or understand how we can even have a relationship with Him when we are so wretched and undeserving. If our relationship with God were a contract, we would have to offer something of equal value to Him as what we were receiving in order to enter into the contract. This is quite obviously not possible. But with a covenant, each party brings to the relationship what they have and gives it all. We give our sinful lives and our fleshly being and receive from God eternal salvation and a new spirit— the Holy Spirit. When discussing the giving of the Holy Spirit with believers I find it very interesting that the language used is that of the father/child relationship.

Now suppose one of you fathers is asked by his son for a fish; he will not give him a snake instead of a fish, will he? Or *if* he is asked for an egg, he will not give him a scorpion, will he? If you then, being evil, know how to give good gifts to your children, how much more shall *your* heavenly Father give the Holy Spirit to those who ask Him?[xlvi][xlvii]

How does all of this talk of covenants relate specifically to parenting? The simple explanation of covenant parenting is this:

> In all things go first to the Bible. If God makes it clear what He would have me do, I do that. If the Bible is silent on a topic, I look not to "nature," but to the natural to see how God designed it to be. There will always be some things unique to each individual child that are not addressed in the Bible and for which there is no example for me to follow. In those situations I believe God has made me the mother of my child and has fully equipped me to determine how best to handle the situation.

I still research to learn new skills or read to see what alternatives have been presented, but I am the expert on my child and that is why God is holding me responsible for the choices I make.[xlviii] I believe that we are to follow God's example in all things. If our heavenly Father is in covenant with us, then we are to be in covenant with our children. We are the first "God" to our children and it is through how they perceive us that they will understand God. How many people have a difficult, if not impossible, time entering into a relationship with God because their earthly father was either absent or abusive and they simply do not understand God as a father? We have a heavy responsibility for our children to present them with a true picture of God through who we are in relationship with them. Thus, if we are in covenant relationship with our children, we will prepare them for covenant relationship with God.

This means that we take everything that we are and have and put it at risk for the sake of the relationship with our children. Whether our children have anything to give back or not, and in the beginning all they have to give is their love and their neediness, we sacrifice all for them. Grace-Based Discipline is part of our covenant obligation to our children.

I know this is not a popular suggestion for those raised in our very individualistic and selfish Western culture. It is, in fact, completely counter-cultural. But God never ordained Western culture or the way it does things, any more than He has any other culture. God wants to impose His heavenly culture on all of our earthly cultures and bring them closer to what He would have them be. Many of the things that our culture offers for childbirth and child raising are counterproductive in raising children for the Lord. This is why it is dangerous to attempt to justify Western culture ideas through Scripture.

I believe that everyone God brings into a person's life is there for a purpose. God uses people and circumstances to help us grow closer to His ideal for us. It is true that He meets you where you are, but He never intends to leave you there. This is also true of our children. Children require constant sacrifice on our part. How strongly this goes against our flesh! "This is My commandment, that you love one another, just as I have loved you. Greater love has no one than this, that one lay down his life for his friends."[xlix] We are called to love our children as Christ has loved us.

I have never grown so much as a person or in my walk with the Lord as when I have listened to that still, small voice inside me prompting me to meet my child's needs when I thought I had nothing else to give. We will all have times when our desire is to strike out at our child. Our frustrations will rise in us and we will have violent feelings. This is normal. But when we can find it in ourselves to stop and give our child a hug we are learning to sacrifice. And when that sacrifice creates better behavior in a child, contrary to what our feelings would have us believe, we are learning from the Holy Spirit a better way to parent. Sacrificing for someone who takes all and gives little is not easy. There would be sufficient grounds for breaking the contract; these are not grounds for breaking the covenant. Just the continued requirement on me as a mother to give all I have to give for the other member of this covenant. The greater is called to serve the weak. The first is called to be last and to put the last first. I am called to make my child a disciple, not a slave.

It is constantly amazing to me that Biblical principles are applied to the Christian walk but somehow fail to be applied to Christian parenting. Christian parenting discussions have been stuck in

Victorian England and have centered around looking up the concepts of "rod," "discipline," "punishment," "obedience," "chastisement," etc. In Victorian England, these were the words that were at the foundation for most Christians' understanding of the entire Christian walk so of course they were to be applied to parenting in a Christian home. We now understand the importance of looking to concepts such as "grace," "love," "servanthood," and "sacrifice" in our understanding of Christianity. It is time to apply these concepts to our parenting.

When these ideas are applied to parenting what emerges is a beautiful picture of parents modeling God's love to their children. Grace, love, servanthood, and sacrifice are the foundations of Grace-Based Discipline. Godly parenting is about being kind and firm, teaching and correcting, respecting and being respected in a way that can only come from relationship. It is from this foundation that you will be able to raise children who are prepared for all of the relationships in their lives as well as the mature covenant relationships of marriage and salvation. Exercising Grace-Based Discipline is a long-term investment in your child.

Appendix A

The Punitive to Positive
Testimony of Joan Sewell

I am a conservative, KJV only, fundamental believer. I have four children ranging from ages two through nine. I have two boys and two girls. I homeschool my kids so I am with them twenty-four hours a day, seven days a week.

Three of my kids are very strong willed. The older three have been spanked according to instruction by those who say not to spank out of anger, making sure the child understands what they are being spanked for, giving a certain amount of swats with a switch (bendable stick), consistently, with prayer, hugging afterwards, not leaving marks, etc. In other words, we have done it as close to the supposed "right" way as anyone could.

My oldest turned nine a few months back and I noticed that we were still dealing with the same old issues with him. He did not seem to be learning internal control. It still took external control to make him obey. This caused me to take a step back and re-evaluate our methods. Did I want my son to discipline my grandchildren the same way I disciplined him? My time is half over with him living in the home under my authority, was I happy with where we were headed? Was I willing to truly change things and try to help him think for himself and not have me do all of his thinking for him? Could I give up the control? Could I allow the Holy Spirit to take over without thinking I had to help? Did I want my other kids to be this way at nine? Was there anything I could do to help the younger ones learn more self-control, self-discipline, and internal motivation by this age? It was about this time that I learned of an online group who were Christians, but did not believe in spanking or any other form of punitive discipline.

I began to question them. I fully expected that I would not receive satisfactory answers and would be about my merry, spanking way. But, deep down, I had never felt completely right about spanking my children. I always felt guilty for this, thinking I was being rebellious to the Proverbs "rod" verses. Since I am a literalist, I did not want to be going against Scripture in any area of my life, but especially in this area because my children are my legacy and most precious gifts.

I began to search myself, talk to my kids, read my Bible, pray, and seek out the answers on this issue without bias. I had read every popular author that was FOR spanking over the years and did not think it was even Christian to NOT believe in spanking. I could see the human logic, but not the Biblical basis for such a belief. I also felt that if someone did not spank, they must be permissive.

I knew that I could read a lot of men's opinions, but the final analysis would come down to one thing: What does God say about this in His Word? One of the first things that struck me was that there were no examples of children being spanked in the Bible. It seemed that if it were that important, then surely God would have elaborated a little more. I started to study the word "rod" or "shebet" so that I could have a thorough understanding of these verses. I began to think about how Jesus dealt with children while on earth and how He deals with us as His children. I thought of all of the scriptures that exhort us to be kind, tender hearted, merciful, joyful, gentle, etc. I started to wonder why these verses did not seem to apply to dealing with our kids in the eyes of a lot of Christians. Yet Jesus personified these qualities toward us. He was over us, yet He was a servant. I questioned the place of grace in the parenting realm. God started showing me so much more than I ever thought possible.

Spanking is no longer an option in this household. Now, we are free to build real and lasting relationships with our kids. These relationships are built on mutual respect and honesty. This is a respect that says, "I will do unto you as I would have you do unto me." I have children who must respect one another and keep their hands to themselves. Just because you are bigger or someone wrongs you does not mean you can hit him or her. Yet I could not seem to get this across before. When my kids wronged us (and ultimately we would tell them, God), we spanked (hit) them. Of course, we always tried to say that spanking was not the same as hitting. Talk about splitting hairs!

It is a journey to truly knowing our children. We are now set free to show them Christ and let Him control their lives. I want my children to see God as a parent who they can turn to in time of need and never be ashamed to run boldly to His throne. They need to respect God, but they also need to see Him as their El Shaddai and serve him because they love Him, not just out of fear. The Bible says perfect love casteth out all fear. I cannot love them as unconditionally as God does, but I can point them to Him and try to model as closely as possible how Jesus gently shepherds us. Isn't that who we are supposed to conform to? We are conforming to the image of Christ. I want my child to focus on Him and not on me as the ultimate example. You have heard the saying, "If you love something, set it free." My children are now allowed the same liberty in Christ that their parents have. It has caused me to draw closer to Him, so that I may know Him better to depend on His wisdom and answers in the daily issues of life instead of the quick and temporary fix of punitive discipline. It is amazing what God can do when we are not standing in His way!

Appendix B[1]

A Scriptural Study of "Rod"

The "Rod" or "Shebet": An In-depth Examination

A close examination of the "rod" scriptures in Proverbs:

Which verses are being referred to as the "rod" scriptures?

Pr 13:24 *He that spareth his rod hateth his son: but he that loveth him chasteneth him betimes.*

Pr 22:15 *Foolishness is bound in the heart of a child; but the rod of correction shall drive it far from him.*

Pr 23:13 *Withhold not correction from the child: for if thou beatest him with the rod, he shall not die.*

---

[1] Compiled by Joan Sewell.

Pr 23:14 *Thou shalt beat him with the rod, and shalt deliver his soul from hell.*

Pr 29:15 *The rod and reproof give wisdom: but a child left to himself bringeth his mother to shame.*

The word rod is "shebet" in Hebrew. This word is defined as following in Strong's Hebrew Lexicon #7626:

> rod, staff, branch, offshoot, club, sceptre, tribe
> a. rod, staff
> b. shaft (of spear, dart)
> c. club (of shepherd's implement)
> d. truncheon, sceptre (mark of authority)
> e. clan, tribe

Strong's definition: From an unused root probably meaning to branch off; a scion, for example literally a stick (for punishing, writing, fighting, walking, ruling, etc.) or figuratively a clan.

King James Word Usage

> tribe 140, rod 34, sceptre 10, staff 2, miscellaneous 4

Matteh is another Hebrew word for rod. This word can mean branch as a vine and is not used here. Maqqel, which has no meaning that can be applied here, is not used in this scripture anyway. Choter, another Hebrew word, means branch, twig, rod and is not used here.

Therefore, the focus is on shebet.

There are 31 other scriptures using this word, translated "rod" in the KJV. These verses will be grouped into categories according to how the word "rod" (translated from "shebet") is used.

THE ROD OF A SHEEP HERDER OR AS AN INSTRUMENT OR TOOL

Leviticus 27:32: *And concerning the tithe of the herd, or of the flock, even of whatsoever passeth under the rod, the tenth shall be holy unto the LORD.*

Psalm 23:4: *Yea, though I walk through the valley of the shadow of death, I will fear no evil: for thou art with me; thy rod and thy staff they comfort me.*

Psalm 2:9: *Thou shalt break them with a rod of iron; thou shalt dash them in pieces like a potter's vessel.*

Isaiah 28:27: *For the fitches are not threshed with a threshing instrument, neither is a cart wheel turned about upon the cummin; but the fitches are beaten out with a staff, and the cummin with a rod.*

Exodus 21:20: *And if a man smite his servant, or his maid, with a rod, and he die under his hand; he shall be surely punished.*

SYMBOLIZING DIRECT HERITAGE FROM GOD (offshoot)

Psalm 74:2: *Remember thy congregation, which thou hast purchased of old; the rod of thine inheritance, which thou hast redeemed; this mount Zion, wherein thou hast dwelt.*

Jeremiah 10:16*: The portion of Jacob is not like them: for he is the former of all things; and Israel is the rod of his inheritance: The LORD of hosts is his name.*

Jeremiah 51:19*: The portion of Jacob is not like them; for he is the former of all things: and Israel is the rod of his inheritance: the LORD of hosts is his name.*

SYMBOLIZING THE AUTHORITY OF THE WICKED

Psalm 125:3*: For the rod of the wicked shall not rest upon the lot of the righteous; lest the righteous put forth their hands unto iniquity.*

Proverbs 22:8*: He that soweth iniquity shall reap vanity: and the rod of his anger shall fail.*

A ROD TO BE USED ON A FOOL

(Fool meaning stupid or silly, literally meaning fat...has a connotation of cocky)

Proverbs 10:13: *In the lips of him that hath understanding wisdom is found: but a rod is for the back of him that is void of understanding.*

Proverbs 26:3: *A whip for the horse, a bridle for the ass, and a rod for the fool's back.*

SYMBOLIZING MAN'S AUTHORITY

II Samuel 7:14: *I will be his father, and he shall be my son. If he commit iniquity, I will chasten him with the rod of men, and with the stripes of the children of men.*

Ezekiel 19:11: *And she had strong rods for the sceptres of them that bare rule, and her stature was exalted among the thick branches, and she appeared in her height with the multitude of her branches.*

Ezekiel 19:14: *And fire is gone out of a rod of her branches, which hath devoured her fruit, so that she hath no strong rod to be a sceptre to rule. This is a lamentation, and shall be for a lamentation.*

SYMBOLIZING GOD'S AUTHORITY

Job 9:34: *Let him take his rod away from me, and let not his fear terrify me.*

Job 21:9: *Their houses are safe from fear, neither is the rod of God upon them.*

Psalm 89:32: *Then will I visit their transgression with the rod, and their iniquity with stripes.*

Isaiah 10:5: *O Assyrian, the rod of mine anger, and the staff in their hand is mine indignation.*

Isaiah 10:15: *Shall the axe boast itself against him that heweth therewith? or shall the saw magnify itself against him that shaketh it? as if the rod should shake itself against them that lift it up, or as if the staff should lift up itself, as if it were no wood.*

Isaiah 11:4: *But with righteousness shall he judge the poor, and reprove with equity for the meek of the earth: and he shall smite the earth with the rod of his mouth, and with the breath of his lips shall he slay the wicked.*

Lamentations 3:1: *I am the man that hath seen affliction by the rod of his wrath.*

Micah 7:14: *Feed thy people with thy rod, the flock of thine heritage, which dwell solitarily in the wood, in the midst of Carmel: let them feed in Bashan and Gilead, as in the days of old.*

Ezekiel 20:37: *And I will cause you to pass under the rod, and I will bring you into the bond of the covenant.*

Ezekiel 21:10: *It is sharpened to make a sore slaughter; it is furbished that it may glitter: should we then make mirth? it contemneth the rod of my son, as every tree.*

Ezekiel 21:13: *Because it is a trial, and what if the sword condemn even the rod? It shall be no more, saith the Lord GOD.*

SYMBOLIZING THE AUTHORITY OF A NATION

Isaiah 9:4: *For thou hast broken the yoke of his burden, and the staff of his shoulder, the rod of his oppressor, as in the day of Midian.*

Isaiah 14:29: *Rejoice not thou, whole Palestina, because the rod of him that smote thee is broken: for out of the serpent's root shall come forth a cockatrice, and his fruit shall be a fiery flying serpent.*

Isaiah 30:31: *For through the voice of the LORD shall the Assyrian be beaten down, which smote with a rod.*

Appendix B[1]

Micah 5:1: *Now gather thyself in troops, O daughter of troops: he hath laid siege against us: they shall smite the judge of Israel with a rod upon the cheek.*

Thus all 36 places where the word "rod" is used in the KJV has been recorded in conjunction with the full counsel of God.

There are only a few places that "shebet" is possibly referring to a literal rod in connection with hitting someone.

First let us look at Exodus 21:20:

Exodus 21:20: *And if a man smite his servant, or his maid, with a rod, and he die under his hand; he shall be surely punished.*

This scripture in Exodus says that if this rod were used on a maid or servant and killed them that it was punishable. So, one can see that it had to be a heavy duty instrument capable of killing someone which would be consistent with the idea of a staff or club. If it is okay to spank a child using this instrument, then it is not mentioned here and if it were, then the child could die by its use.

Next, one should examine the meaning of "the stripes of the children of men" in II Samuel 7:14:

II Samuel 7:14: *I will be his father, and he shall be my son. If he commit iniquity, I will chasten him with the rod of men, and with the stripes of the children of men.*

Here is a lengthy quote from Matthew Henry's commentary on this particular verse:

> I will be his father, and he shall be my son. We need no more to make us and ours happy than to have God to be a Father to us and them; and all those to whom God is a Father he by his grace makes his sons, by giving them the disposition of children. If he be a careful, tender, bountiful Father to us, we must be obedient, tractable, dutiful children to him. The promise here speaks as unto sons. [1.] That his Father would correct him when there was occasion; for what son is he whom the Father chasteneth not? Afflictions are an article of the covenant, and are not only consistent with, but flow from, God's fatherly love. "If he commit iniquity, as it proved he did (1 Ki. 11:1), I will chasten him to bring him to repentance, but it shall be with the rod of men, such a rod as men may wield—I will not plead against him with the great power of God,'' Job 23:6. Or rather such a rod as men may bear —"I will consider his frame, and correct him with all possible tenderness and compassion when there is need, and no more than there is need of; it shall be with the stripes, the touches (so the word is) of the children of men; not a stroke, or wound, but a gentle touch.'' [2.] That yet he would not disinherit him (v. 15): My mercy (and that is the inheritance of sons) shall not depart from him. The revolt of the ten tribes from the

house of David was their correction for iniquity, but the constant adherence of the other two to that family, which was a competent support of the royal dignity, perpetuated the mercy of God to the seed of David, according to this promise; though that family was cut short, yet it was not cut off, as the house of Saul was. Never any other family swayed the sceptre of Judah than that of David. This is that covenant of royalty celebrated (Ps. 89:3, etc.) as typical of the covenant of redemption and grace. 2. Others of them relate to Christ, who is often called David and the Son of David, that Son of David to whom these promises pointed and in whom they had their full accomplishment. He was of the seed of David, Acts 13:23. To him God gave the throne of his father David (Lu. 1:32), all power both in heaven and earth, and authority to execute judgment. He was to build the gospel temple, a house for God's name, Zec. 6:12, 13. That promise, I will be his Father, and he shall be my Son, is expressly applied to Christ by the apostle, Heb. 1:5. But the establishing of his house, and his throne, and his kingdom, for ever (v. 13, and again, and a third time v. 16. for ever), can be applied to no other than Christ and his kingdom. David's house and kingdom have long since come to an end; it is only the Messiah's kingdom that is everlasting, and of the increase of his government and peace there shall be no end. The supposition of committing iniquity cannot indeed be applied to the Messiah himself, but it is applicable (and very comfortable) to his spiritual seed. True believers have their infirmities, for which they may expect to be corrected, but they shall not be cast off. Every transgression in the covenant will not throw us out of covenant. Now, (1.) This message Nathan faithfully delivered to David (v. 17); though, in forbidding him to build the temple, he contradicted his own words, yet he was not backward to do it when he was better informed concerning the mind of God. (2.) These promises God faithfully performed to David and his seed in due time. Though David came short of making good his purpose to build God a house, yet God did not come short of making good his promise to build him a house. Such is the tenour of the covenant we are under; though there are many failures in our performances, there are none in God's.

When one observes the use of the rod on fools, this would be adults who are "fools" because they are grown and still have no self-control. It would be comparable to a criminal being beaten. This is not speaking of a young child. There are examples of criminals being beaten in Scripture. There are NO examples of children being beaten with any rod.

In most other instances the word "rod" is used to symbolize God's authority or the authority of a nation.

SYMBOLIZING THE AUTHORITY OF PARENTS

Upon reading the "shebet" passages in Proverbs, one will notice that you can always substitute the word "authority" for "rod." "Rod" is referring to God's authority and the authority of nations in the above verses. Thus, the word "rod" is referring to a parent's authority in all five of the Proverbs references, including the following verses:

Pr 23:13: *Withhold not correction from the child: for if thou beatest him with the rod, he shall not die.*

Pr 23:14: *Thou shalt beat him with the rod, and shalt deliver his soul from hell.*

In the preceding verses, one can see that the child shall not die with this rod. Yet in Exodus, we saw that a man COULD cause someone to die with a literal shebet. If Scripture were talking about a literal rod here, this would be a contradiction because it says he SHALL NOT die. A person cannot kill another with their authority. They can be striking (beating) the other person with their authority by using their authority to discipline (teach, disciple, educate, instruct) and guide them.

IF this scripture were referring to a literal beating, taken in context, it would have to be speaking about a grown child. The verses before and after Proverbs

23:13-14 were written by a father who was instructing his adolescent son. However, one still has the problem of the contradiction as far as whether or not a "shebet" can cause someone to die.

Another observation worth mention is the Hebrew word translated "child" in the "rod" Scriptures of Proverbs.

This word is "na'ar".

Meaning of "na'ar":

aboy,lad,servant,youth,retainer
a.boy,lad,youth
b. servant, retainer

Concretely a boy (as active), from the age of infancy to adolescence; by implication a servant; also (by interchange of sex) a girl (of similar latitude in age).

The KJV translates it as follows:

young man 76, servant 54, child 44, lad 33, young 15, children 7, youth 6, babe 1, boys 1

This word "na'ar" is referring to boys most of the time (since a lad would be a male) and usually young men.

Therefore, *if* one took these scriptures to mean literal physical punishment, then it would possibly only apply to fathers spanking their sons who are older (since adolescence can go through the early 20's). Most Christian discipline "experts" do not mention this. Yet, if one is to interpret this verse literally, this would have to be the explanation. Law-based Christian parenting authors say a parent should be able to STOP spanking by the time their children reach 12 or 13, yet according to this scripture, this parent would not even START using physical punishment until then. These verses, if taken literally, would be referring to this form of punishment as an absolute last resort to save the child (which was possibly a boy only) from hell.

Many Christians have taken FIVE verses and hung a whole child-rearing philosophy on them! Parents are told to use this as a primary form of punishment (what these experts refer to as discipline). Some use the word "punishment" and the term "discipline" interchangeably when they mean two entirely different things. These people are basing their theology on nothing more than the traditions of men!

Further, we are told in Deuteronomy 21:18-21:

18 If a man have a stubborn and rebellious son, which will not obey the voice of his father, or the voice of his mother, and that, when they have chastened him, will not   hearken   untothem:
19 Then shall his father and his mother lay hold on him, and bring him out unto the elders of his city, and unto the   gateofhisplace;
20 And they shall say unto the elders of his city, This our son is stubborn and rebellious, he will not obey our voice; heisaglutton,andadrunkard.

21 And all the men of his city shall stone him with stones, that he die: so shalt thou put evil away from among you; and all Israel shall hear, and fear.

The parents are told first to talk to their child (he has not heard their voice). Then, they are told to chasten him. Chasten simply means correct with words or blows. It seems they were supposed to instruct, then correct him if he did not heed their verbal correction. Then, if this does not work, he is to be stoned.

If we are no longer to stone, then why do we assume we should use physical beatings to bring about repentance? Shouldn't we make examples of a few children and stone them too? Why were they to go ahead and stone them to death if they would not repent and be obedient? This was because the Holy Spirit was not actively convicting hearts and they did not yet have direct access to God.

Jesus said in the case of the adulterous woman to let him who was without sin cast the first stone. Parents don't stone their kids because the parents themselves are just as much a sinner as their rebellious child.

Jesus was gentle with children. He is a shepherd to the sheep. The shepherd uses HIS rod to guide the sheep, not to beat them! Psalm 23 uses "shebet" to describe the shepherd's "rod." People have mentioned to this author that the shepherd would use his "rod" to break the legs of a wandering sheep to keep it from going away and getting hurt, so this is proof of how we should physically punish our children. However, this only proves that we should try to keep our children's hearts on the right path by praying for God to convict and protect them. He is the GREAT Shepherd and He will work in their lives in a much more effective manner than we can. If He chooses to allow some kind of circumstance or situation (to break their legs) in their life, to keep them in the fold, then so be it! He is much stronger than human parents. Our children's "legs can be broken" by natural, spiritual, and logical consequences (which God allows in their lives) even more effectively than by man-made pain.

Bibliography

Abrams, Rabbi Judith Z. and Dr. Steven A. Jewish Parenting: Rabbinic Insights. Jason Aronson, Inc., New Jersey: 1994.

Acredolo, Linda, PhD., and Susan Goodwyn, PhD. Baby Signs. Contemporary Books, Chicago: 1996.

Budd, Linda S., Ph.D. Living with the Active Alert Child: Groundbreaking Strategies for Parents. Parenting Press, Inc., Washington: 1993.

Campbell, D. Ross, M.D. How to Really Love Your Child. SP Publications, USA: 1977.

De Guyter, Aldine. Breastfeeding: Biocultural Perspectives. Hawthorne, NY: 1995.

Elkin, Frederick, and Handel, Gerald. The Child and Society: The Process of Socialization. Random House, USA: 1960.

Ginott, Dr. Haim G. Between Parent & Child. Avon Books, New York: 1956.

Kippley, Sheila. Breastfeeding and Natural Child Spacing: The Ecology of Natural Mothering. Penguin Books, NY: 1974.

Kuzara Seibold, Lisa, M.Ed. Wonderfully Made: A Training Manual for Volunteer and Staff Teachers of Preschool, Pre-Kindergarten and Kindergarten Children: 1997.

Martin, Robert J. <u>Teaching Through Encouragement: Techniques to Help Students Learn</u>. Prentice Hall, Inc., New Jersey: 1980.

Montagu, Ashley. <u>Touching: The Human Significance of the Skin</u>. Harper & Row, New York: 1971.

Sears, William, M.D. <u>Nighttime Parenting</u>. La Leche League International, USA: 1985.

Sears, William, M.D., and Martha Sears, R.N. <u>Parenting the Fussy Baby and High-Need Child</u>. Little, Brown and Company, U.S.A.: 1996.

Tate, W. Randolph. <u>Biblical Interpretation</u>. Hendrickson Publishers, Inc., U.S.A.: 1997.

Vannoy, Steven W. <u>The Ten Greatest Gifts I Give My Children</u>. Simon & Schuster, USA: 1994.

End Notes

[i] All Bible verses are taken from the New American Standard Bible. AMG Publishers. Chattanooga, TN 37422. USA: 1960.

[ii] Montagu, Ashley. Touching. pp 142-143.

[iii] Montagu, Ashley. Touching. pp 143-144.

[iv] Sears, William.:1986 pp 38-42.

[v] Christians still die physically, but I am referring to spiritual death.

[vi] Matthew 5.21-22.

[vii] Proverbs 22.6.

[viii] 2 Timothy 3.16-17.

[ix] Matthew 28.19-20.

[x] Deuteronomy 21.18-21.

[xi] See Matthew 26.36-40.

[xii] Lattore, Pat. Leadership. Fuller Theological Seminary, 1997.

[xiii] Covey, Steven. Seven Habits of Highly Successful People. Simon & Schuster, New York: 1990. Covey has applied this concept, and each of the other six, to families in his more recent book Seven Habits of Highly Successful Families.

[xiv] Genesis 1.28.

[xv] 2 Timothy 2.13.

[xvi] Galations 5.22.

[xvii] Leviticus 19.2.

[xviii] Ephesians 5.7.

[xix] Matthew 5.23-24.

[xx] Genesis 1.27.

[xxi] Acts 17.22-34.

[xxii] See the works of Dr. James Clark Maloney and Breastfeeding: Biocultural Perspectives. Aldine De Guyter, 1995: Hawthorne, NY.

[xxiii] See Breastfeeding: Biocultural Perspectives. Aldine De Guyter, 1995: Hawthorne, NY.

[xxiv] The Greek word "peotho" means "to persuade, to win over, to be persuaded, to listen to, to obey" and is closely related etymologically to the word "pisterio" meaning "to trust." The difference in meaning comes from the understanding that obedience is an act which naturally comes out of trust.

[xxv] Proverbs 23.13.

[xxvi] Please see Appendix "B" for a more complete study of the "rod" verses.

[xxvii] Esther 4.11

[xxviii] Deuteronomy 21.18-21.

[xxix] Matthew 18.21-35.

[xxx] Ephesians 6.1-3.

[xxxi] Ephesians 6.4.

[xxxii] In secular circles this style might be called "democratic" or "authoritative," however it is revealed in Scripture

as the style by which God parents believers. Grace-Based Discipline is based on the model God gives us in Scripture.

[xxxiii] Natural Consequences occur unless they are prevented. God has set them in nature to teach lessons. It is a parent's job to determine if a child is ready to experience a consequence or not. If not, block it. If so, let it happen and allow them to learn. If there is no natural consequence then I question whether there needs to be one. I do not teach Logical Consequences which tend to be punitive.

[xxxiv] John 14.6.

[xxxv] Elkin, Frederick and Gerald Handel. The Child and Society. Random House, New York: 1960. p 35.

[xxxvi] See Sears The Baby Book; The Discipline Book; The Fussy Baby and High Need Child Book.

[xxxvii] I am grateful to Joanne Davidson for this tool and many others for which I will give her credit.

[xxxviii] I alter between male and female gender references. This is not to imply that any tool is more effective for either boys or girls. A tools effectiveness will be determined by your child's temperament, personalities and interests.

[xxxix] Time-Out is a punitive act with the same results—or lack thereof—as spanking and all other punishment.

[xl] Joanne Davidson.

[xli] Joanne Davidson. This is an adaptation of Jane Nelson's Positive Time Out.

[xlii] Joanne Davidson.

[xliii] Genesis 2.24.

[xliv] John 14.7 (italics added).

[xlv] 2 Timothy 2.13.

[xlvi] Luke 11.11-13.

[xlvii] It is the repeated use in Scripture of examples from the natural to illustrate what God would do or have us do that gives me confidence in looking to the natural as God designed it when the Bible is silent on a subject.

[xlviii] These concepts also apply to my husband. I am not excluding him or lessening his importance in child-raising, I am simply speaking for myself.

[xlix] John 15.12-13.

Acknowledgements

There are so many people I want to thank. I will start with Lisa Kuzara Seibold who mentored me and not only taught me much about non-punitive discipline but much about myself as well. I am grateful to all of the women involved in the Positive Christian AP list and AMU who were my support and my online community during the writing of this book. Thank you also to Shannon Smith for all of her help in early editing and for being such a supportive friend at a critical time during the writing of this book; Tonya Pearsall and her family; and Joanne Davidson and her family who are my friends and my support where I live. I am especially grateful to Joanne for all of her practical GBD ideas. I owe so much to my mother and father who raised me with the foundation onto which God could write all of what I've learned. Thank you also to my husband William and our children Liam and Fiona who supported me in all of the time and energy that completing this book required. Of course, thank you to my dedicated editor Vicki Schmitz who really "got" what I was trying to say, and to my publisher Rebecca Beck. Mostly I owe my eternal gratitude to my Savior who has extended grace to me and taught me how to extend it to my children.

About the Author

Crystal Lutton is a 30-year-old mother of 2 who has devoted most of her life to working with children and learning non-punitive methods for parenting. She is the Pastor of Arms of Love Family Fellowship, an AP friendly home church where families are encouraged to worship together. She does much personal, relationship, and parenting counseling online and is co-owner of an E-Groups list for Positive Christian AP where Christian women are encouraged in their efforts to practice AP and Grace-Based Discipline with their children. Crystal received her Master of Arts in Theology from Fuller Theological Seminary and has searched Scripture for God's heart for families. *Biblical Parenting* is the product of her theological studies and her practical experience using and teaching non-punitive discipline.